SPECIAL LOVE

From Mogoloid to Developmentally Disabled
Or
A Gift in a Damaged Package

Carl F. Smith

Copyright © 2014 Authored By Carl F. Smith
All rights reserved.

ISBN: 1500523461
ISBN 13: 9781500523466

This book is dedicated to all the special people who gave Carlton a voice by being part of his life

SPECIAL LOVE

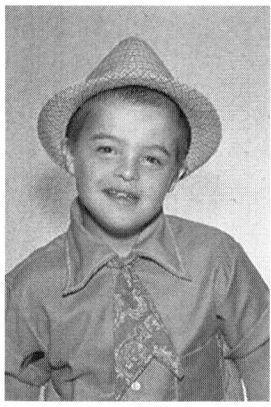

My favorite picture of Carlton age 12

My wife Mimi and I have been fortunate over the years because we have received so much Special Love. This love came from our family, our friends and especially from our severely retarded son Carlton. Carlton was born in 1959. We were told he was a mongoloid. We were completely unaware of just what a mongoloid was, but judging from the grim faces at the hospital we knew it wasn't too good. All we knew was that Carlton was quiet and cute so like any new parents we were elated but concerned. As knowledge of retardation increased, Carlton was rediagnosed as Downes Syndrome. After Carlton's birth we were blessed with three other children, Colleen, Tom and Alicia.

As a baby Carlton was hardly any different than any other child. In fact the differences Carlton had as a baby were differences many new parents dream of: he was slower and quieter because he never talked. He never really cried much either. His grandparents lived close by as did his Uncle Jerry and Aunt Aljeanne, so Mimi and I had a lot of support and were surrounded by Special Love.

When our family was young we decided to take Carlton, his sister and his brother, (daughter Alicia was yet to be born) to Buffalo, New York to visit their grandparents. We traveled in our VW Bug. Talk about something special, that trip not only brought us Special Love, it brought special hate, special fatigue, special patience and a special sense that anyone who would drive three thousand miles in a VW Bug with three kids in diapers and on bottles had to be out of their minds. To this day my wife and I believe that that trip cemented our marriage, nothing we could have done since could bring us to the emotional pitch that we attained driving across country as one happy family. The return trip involved Mimi and Tommy flying back from Chicago.

After that trip we were still getting plenty of advice but little actual help. As our family grew, things became a little hectic. We looked around for a program that might help us. There weren't many programs for severely handicapped youngsters in the early sixties. We found nothing in Crestline the small mountain town where we were living, but we did locate one in San Bernardino, a twisting fourteen-mile drive on a two-lane highway. Mimi and a couple of other parents managed to get there for a while, but schedules changed and Mimi became pregnant with Alicia so we were back to step one. We needed help, we needed Special Love. In walked a handful of friends named Laura, Kathy and a Mr. Costillo. Laura and Cathy picked Carlton up every morning and took him to his School of Hope; Mr. Costillo transported him home every afternoon.

I got a letter last week from Mr. Costillo's son Derek. He was in the seminary for the past eight years but decided the priesthood was not for him. He since has married and now hopes to become a social worker in San Diego. He'll be a good one because he learned Special Love from his dad who showed a young couple what love was all about by bringing their son home each day from his School that offered us hope.

Carlton had to leave for a State Hospital when he was eight years old because with three children and Carlton, who wasn't healthy, we were unable to function as a family. My wife's health was affected too and although we had a great deal of support, our situation was getting desperate. We could find no one to help us with our son and our problems. It's difficult when a child leaves home at any age but when Carlton left home; it was probably the most difficult day of our lives.

In time however he was placed in the home of a very special lady whose name was Gladys. Gladys loved Carlton back to health with her own brand of Special Love. Eventually Gladys too was overwhelmed by all the demands made upon her and she had to give up the challenged children she had grown to love so much. She called me and very sadly told me of her decision. And so, Carlton moved to Hilldale a residential facility where he lived for the rest of his life.

While Carlton lived at Hilldale, Mimi and I remained involved with his care. We started a parent group so that everyone who was involved with our child realized that Carlton was part of a family, a mother, father, two sisters and a brother who loved him dearly. We saw good things and we saw bad. We saw so much Special Love by people during those twenty years that our heads are still spinning. We met teachers, dentists, pediatricians, parents, aides, nurses, volunteers and social workers who have laughed and cried with us throughout the years, they all had a special place in their hearts for Carlton because Carlton and people like him brought out the best in people. I have never seen a person like Carlton who without ever saying a word had managed to make so many people feel loved and wanted- that's Special Love. We stayed in touch with Hilldale long after Carlton's death. .

We had one young man living at Hilldale named Lou. Lou was Carlton's friend. He would bend down in his wheel chair and roll a ball toward Carlton. Carlton would roll it back and they would both laugh at each other. Rolling a ball was all it took to form a lifelong friendship. Again, Special Love. When Lou had a good day, which meant a day when he didn't scratch or harm himself, he got to call us up on the telephone. Lou called about three times a week. Sometimes I didn't feel like talking to Lou because I didn't understand him too well. When Lou called I talked because I knew that Lou tried hard so he could talk to someone who loved him. I also realized that Lou didn't really have anyone else he could call. At last I began to understand what Lou was saying. All Lou ever said was "Hi

Carlton's Dad". My simple proximity to my son gave me the gift of Special Love from Lou.

Yes! Love reaches out! Carlton's sisters have both worked with the retarded or Developmentally Disabled as they are called today. Lou still calls us and people still come and involve themselves at Hilldale. They give their Special Love to those who can't do a whole lot for themselves but I can guarantee you, they are getting it back one hundred fold.

What I've learned over the years is that each one of us has some kind of unique Special Love to share with others. The thing we have to do is share it-- not later on-- but now--today. This week give a friend a listen, write a letter, make a phone call or send a flower. Mimi and I had our Carlton; you all have your own Carltons. Let your Special Love reach out.

Years ago when I was at Grossmont College getting ready to teach a course, a very cute, very young lady came up to me and said she really wanted to meet me just because she knew I was Carlton's father----keep in mind Carlton did not speak… Special Love can be silent.

You know sometimes it's hard for grandmothers and grandfathers and close family to accept the reality of a retarded child. My dad and mom were different. They received Carlton with open arms, just the way he was. Soon after Carlton was born, my dad shared his thoughts about his grandson in the local newspaper. In his weekly article he wrote;

> "This week I am going to knock out a few words about a word that has bothered me for some time. The word is "Retard"- the adjective it builds is the word retarded. In the dictionary it means "hold back, "delay" and other such synonyms. In music, the abbreviation "ret" means "slow, soft and somewhat sweet." I agree with that definition entirely.
>
> I have a grandson who has been pronounced by medical and other people as "retarded." And I guess he is, for he is slow, soft and plenty sweet. To my mind, slowness these days is a virtue, not a drawback. Softness too, is a hard quality to come across — and sweetness, if you find some, put it in a jar, for it is a seldom commodity.

Charley as I call him (his real name is Carlton and he is the son of my son Carl, who teaches school up here and Mimi, who teaches spasmodically between babies) is slow. He doesn't walk too much yet, although his younger sister does. But he will, when the right time comes. He doesn't talk yet — which is a relief as a great many people who have nothing to say talk a great deal — but he will when the right time comes. There is nothing wrong with him physically — and there is nothing wrong with him mentally as far as I can see. He is just "bidin' his time." But he has one quality that a great number of us have had at one time or another, and in the rush of life have tossed aside- the desire to love and to be loved.

I watch him sometimes as he looks out of the window and sees the birds flying and the trees and flowers growing. They do not, I believe amaze him. He accepts them as friends — as things that are and should be there and it is very satisfactory to him. He looks, he listens he studies peculiar little things — and what is going on in his mind is beyond your and my conception. He has his viewpoint, and we have ours. He is happy — very happy. I sometimes wish I could be one third as happy as he is.

I believe that the God who built this world and then populated it with the polyglot collection of flotsam and jetsam we know as the human race, has His own ideas of the way things should operate. I believe he holds in His hands a finely balanced scale — when something is missing on one side, something is put in to compensate for it on the other.

I don't take much truck with folks who turn their heads and say "What a pity?" If they could go to bed one night with the peace of mind Charley possesses, the national crop of ulcers would ultimately die out. I've got a lot of faith in Charley. Whatever was left out for him on one side will be generously supplied on another.

They say it's" Love that makes the world go round." Well, Charley has his own little world and if Love will make it go round, it will spin like a top. Because there's an awful lot of it distributed among his grandpa, his grandma, his pa, his ma, his uncles, aunts and cousins.

Retarded my eye, the kid is "just bidin' his time."

Carlton in an Easter play at The School of Hope 1966

This is the story of Carlton and the changes that took place in his lifetime. It is the story of the Special Love he gave, received and spread to other people much like the flowers he called his friends.

BEGINNINGS

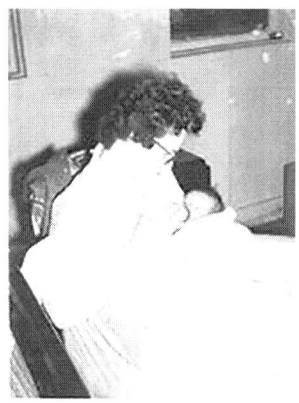

In 1959 my son Carlton came into this world as a severely retarded mongoloid child. Forty years later, beating all odds of survival he left this same world as a developmentally disabled Downe's Syndrome adult. Those forty years tell a story of heartache and joy, success and failure, frustration and change. On the day he was born, my wife Mimi and I were unaware of what lay in store for us with Carlton. At that time mongoloids were usually placed in State Hospitals soon after being diagnosed.

In 1961 Dr. Downes discovered that all mongoloids were born with an extra chromosome. Before 1961 and the discovery of the extra chromosome these type of people were referred to as a mongoloids because of their facial features. Since Doctor Downe's research they were first referred to as Downes Syndrome then just Downes and now persons with Down's Syndrome (the "e" has been dropped however I use the original spelling). Like the rest of the population persons with Downes Syndrome come in many degrees of intelligence. High functioning persons with Downes Syndrome can be found working at super markets, restaurants, schools and anyplace where innovative people see the value of a dedicated worker who can learn to do a job well.

Carlton lived on the low end of the ability spectrum. He managed to get the things he needed to survive. He managed so well that he stayed alive for a little over forty years. His is the story of change. Change from well-intentioned ignorance to scientific understanding. Advances that took a good deal of work on the part of Mimi and me, other parents and a whole myriad of dedicated people. For Mimi and I Carlton changed our lives. Through Mimi and me and countless others Carlton helped change society in its dealings with persons with developmental disabilities. Carlton's story continues today. Medical and behavioral science have made enormous progress into the lives of these developmentally disabled individuals. Society is learning to accept them as they are. This is Carlton's story and it begins shortly after Mimi and I were married in 1958.

FIRST COMES LOVE

We announced our engagement while Mimi was teaching in San Leandro and I was teaching in the San Bernardino Mountains in the town of Crestline at a school camp operated by the Norwalk La Mirada School District. We set the wedding date for June 28th, 1958, in Lancaster, New York. We had a beautiful wedding at St Mary's church followed by a scrumptious homemade wedding brunch and dinner. The reception was still going on long after we left for our honeymoon at a small cottage on Moon Lake in central New York. After a week, at a rental cost of fifteen dollars, we returned to Cortland State Teachers College where I attended summer school to pick up courses I needed for a California teaching credential. We left for California soon after I finished my studies. In route my poor 1950 Ford blew a rod in New Mexico so we proceeded west from there at about thirty miles per hour. We arrived in Crestline where Mimi had signed a contract to teach first grade and where I would return to the school camp. We had spent our last nickel for a coke in Barstow and we were dead broke.

Our first home was an old run down hovel at the entrance of Thousand Pines Baptist Camp near Lake Gregory Village. The Norwalk School District rented the camp during the week for its school program. Our rustic old cabin had been the first school house in the San Bernardino Mountains and had been converted to staff living quarters years before it became our home. The living room was our bedroom. Our bathroom and closet space were located one step down from the living room. Through a large crack in the bathroom wall, we could watch the snow fall and see animals in our yard. The kitchen served as a dining room and laundry room. The front porch pulled away from the rest of the house so jumping from the house to the porch was the norm. The ceiling leaked and we had buckets ready to catch the drips, winter, spring, summer and fall. Three stately pines surrounded our cabin in the woods. A grove of live oak grew nearby. Deer came to the kitchen window. Squirrels and birds brightened the days with their chattering and singing. Despite the cabin's shortcomings, it was a pleasant place to live and would become Carlton's first home.

Mimi was pregnant before we left New York for our new life in California. For the first half of the school year, Mimi would trudge down the hill to catch a ride to her school in the Valley of Enchantment. Being pregnant made the walk up and down the hill good for her according to all the experts on birthing. At the time, most of the female teachers were getting pregnant and Mimi's principal, Don Vinne, had already lost three teachers that year. Mimi dreaded breaking the news about joining her teaching sisters on the road to motherhood. My dad came to her rescue with a card he drew to announce our joyous news to Mr. Vinne.

TIME FOR THE BABY CARRIAGE

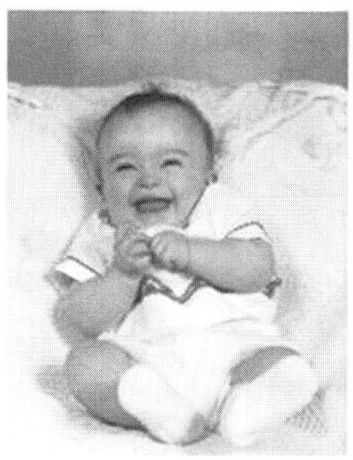

Carlton at about 5 months

As the birth of Carlton approached, our excitement ran high. I felt our unborn child kicking and asked Mimi if she was OK. She assured me that she was fine. The doctor figured Carlton would arrive toward the end of April. Mimi had her overnight bag packed. We could leave at the first sign of a labor pain. We were ready.

Looking back I see how naive we were about the birth of our first child. Making our child was easy, raising him was another story. On April 7, 1959 as Mimi and I sat down to eat our favorite dinner of pork chops with an onion on top smothered in catsup (a delicacy named "Mimi Chops" our grandsons eat to this day) Mimi felt ill. She didn't feel like eating pork chops with an onion on top smothered in catsup that night and she hasn't cared for that particular dish ever since. Dumb as we were, we naturally figured that Mimi's stomach ache signaled the stomach flu. We got into our nearly gasless car, left behind the carefully packed overnight bag and drove to our doctor's office.

Dr. Atkinson, a gentle, kind, easy going general practitioner, happened to be in his office that evening. When he saw Mimi he told us to get to the hospital and assured us that he'd be right behind us. We made a quick stop at the gas station to buy one dollar's worth of gas, just enough to get us to Santa Anita Hospital in Lake Arrowhead.

Feeling the urgency of the situation Mimi urged me to go faster. She yelled "push it." I thought she meant push her stomach. I pushed her stomach. She screamed, "Not my stomach you nut! The car!" I got to the hospital in no time at all. We were greeted by a nurse who quickly helped Mimi into a wheelchair. Twenty minutes after we arrived at Santa Anita Hospital, Dr. Atkinson announced that I was the father of a son. My son was in an incubator but the doctor told me not to worry as Mimi and the baby were both doing fine.

When I went back to the hospital the next day, Mimi was in tears. She told me that a nun came into her room at midnight and asked her what we were going to name our son. He wasn't breathing well so they wanted to baptize him for safekeeping. Mimi told the Sister that our son would be named Carlton Francis. Mimi was terrified. She had many questions but no one had any answers. The nun advised Mimi that no one wants to raise a child that is not perfect so, if anything was wrong with Carlton she should pray for God to take him. Mimi said many prayers in the hours, days, weeks, months and years that followed: not one of those thousands of prayers involved God taking any child much less her own.

Carlton survived that night and seemed to be gaining strength. But the next morning when I saw Dr. Atkinson, he said he thought Carlton might be a Mongoloid. He wasn't sure because he had never seen or delivered a mongoloid before. We had never even heard of a Mongoloid. The next day Carlton was doing better. Dr. Atkinson said he might have been wrong and suggested we have Carlton examined by a specialist after we took him home.

That afternoon my brother brought a thermos full of martinis to the hospital to celebrate Carlton. It was the first happy time we'd had since his birth.

After three days Mimi came home from the hospital. Carlton was still frail and wasn't breathing well enough to leave his incubator. There was nothing we could do but go home and worry about our son. It was difficult taking Mimi home from the hospital without our baby. It was even more difficult visiting him at the hospital during the following weeks. We looked through the glass window and watched, unable to hold our own son. It was a discouraging and foreboding experience. When Carlton could finally leave the hospital, we felt great because we were finally able to hold him.

THE ADVENTURE BEGINS WITH A NOTE

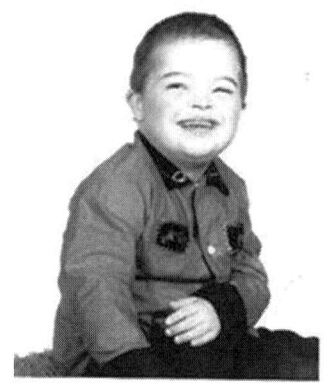

Carlton-3 years old

When Carlton was born there was much confusion about his condition by family members, friends, and Mimi and I. When we broke the news to our loved ones we received many letters full of love and hope. These were the days of what is now call "Snail Mail." Phone calls were expensive so putting words on paper and sending a letter was the way things were done. Our mail box was full. "I am sure with God's grace he will be fine." Mimi's sister wrote. She was right. "I know it will mean an operation but it is one that will be successful" wrote Mimi's mother. Our dear friend Father Mooney's letter turned out to be prophetic: "I think that the important thing is to be sure that one does not get mad at the good Lord. His ways are different from ours but He is blameless. So many times we stress the importance of the body but really it is our soul that is of primary value. We can have eternal happiness no matter what the body happens to be. My prayers are for the parents to have courage and devotion. The boy will be the means of bringing grace untold. That is the Lord's return to unselfishness and acceptance of personal adversities." At the time it was the dark ages for the Developmentally Disables and everyone was clueless.

We took Carlton to Dr. Wilson, a pediatric specialist in San Bernardino, he confirmed Dr. Atkinson's diagnosis. He told us that Carlton was a Mongoloid. I asked what that meant and I wanted to know how he could tell by just looking. The doctor told me that Mongoloids have straight lifelines on the palms of their hands, slanted eyes; ears set a little lower on their heads than other children and no discernable fingerprints. He told us Mongoloids tend to be retarded and have a short life expectancy. Dr. Wilson told us it would be best to place Carlton in a state hospital, the sooner the better and that the name Mongoloid was short for Mongolian Idiot.

We were in no position to argue with the Doctor. We left feeling depressed, angry and alone. We left with a million unanswered questions. Why was Dr. Wilson so sure that Carlton was a Mongoloid by just observing him? Were there other mongoloids? We'd never seen or heard of one. Was Carlton a first? Was there a cure? Why should we put him away and where are these state hospitals?

We looked at Carlton's eyes, ears, fingertips, and the straight lifeline on his tiny hands and wondered if Dr. Wilson was seeing the same child that we were seeing. What a way to diagnose a child! We saw a cute happy little baby and couldn't understand what we had just heard from Dr. Wilson. On the trip back to Crestline we were too confused to talk much but we did try to make some sense out of what we had just experienced.

When we got back home, Mimi and I had a lot of soul searching and discussions about Carlton. We knew we had to find out as much as we could about mongoloids. We realized Carlton was not a strong baby, but was that any reason to give him up? We looked at his diagnostic signs and had a hard time understanding how these physical features, which we hadn't even noticed, could condemn our son to life in a state hospital. We knew nothing about state hospitals. Hospitals were for sick people and Carlton did not seem to be sick.

We didn't know where to begin. We did get a lot of encouragement from my mom and dad and my brother and his family who were living in Crestline. They saw the same child we saw and saw no reason to give him up. Carlton being our first child gave us nothing to compare his development with. He was a slow eater but he drank his bottle at every feeding (a hint of things to come). He slept well and seemed to be a very happy child.

There was another family in Crestline who had a retarded child. Their son, Jimmy, was about ten or eleven and had a twin brother. Jimmy managed very well even though he couldn't attend school. He did, however, hang out at the local elementary school across the street from his house. He seemed to know all the teachers and most of the school kids by name. If this was what Carlton was going to be like Mimi and I were comfortable with it. Seeing Jimmy and having the support of our family made the decision to keep Carlton an easy one.

We still knew little about mongolism but we could find out and be better able to raise our son. So our discussions and soul searching helped us decide to accept Carlton the way he was and listen to our hearts as to how he would be raised.

At the time I was taking courses that I needed to get my teaching credential at University of California Riverside. When I was there for one of my evening classes, I stopped by the library to see what I could find about mongolism. This is what people did in the days before google: they read books. The library was full of books written by learned men and women. Books written by experts. A book was the natural place to look for answers. The library had one book on the subject. The book had pictures and diagrams of ear placement, eye placement, palms of hands, fingers, thumbs, feet and toes. It described the trials and tribulations of Mongolian Idiots. A father of a Mongoloid had placed a hand written note in the front of the book that said, "If you are the parent of a child like this, don't read this book as it is full of misinformation. It does great injustice to these children. Raise your child like you would any other child with loving care." We put the note back, took this father at his word, and raised our son with loving care. Life changing advice from a perfect stranger.

When Carlton came home from the hospital, I set his crib up near the old fashioned steam heater. Like all new parents, we spent most of our time listening, just to make sure that he was breathing.

Mimi carried Carlton everywhere she went until the day I found an old English perambulator with large wheels that had spokes and a black velvet covering in a junk store in the Lake Gregory Village, just down the hill from our cabin. The bed had tie down latches that held it in place when you were pushing the buggy. When you unhooked the latches the bed became a cradle. Carlton spent a great deal of time in his perambulator. Mimi took him on walks through the camp in that buggy and rocked him in its cradle when he was home in the old schoolhouse.

Soon after Carlton was born, we moved into our own home. During Carlton's first year we had no one to compare him to. He was quiet but he did everything other people's children did. He ate, he crawled, he went to the bathroom, he slept and he smiled at us. He just did these things at a slower pace. We left him with baby sitters when we wanted to go out. He didn't need our undivided attention around the clock because Carlton wasn't sick. He was just slow. In many ways, he was an easy child to raise. As he grew, things would change.

My college roommate, Joe, a painting contractor, lived near us in Crestline. One afternoon Mimi and I wanted to get away by ourselves for a few hours. We called Joe and asked him if he'd watch Carlton while we did a little shopping. Joe came right over. Carlton was asleep upstairs when Joe arrived. When we returned home a couple of hours later, Joe was nowhere to be found. We went upstairs. Carlton was in his crib still sound asleep. Mimi telephoned Joe. She asked him how he was doing. Joe said everything was fine. He had left because he really couldn't find anything to do. She asked him about Carlton, There was silence at the other end of the line. Then Joe groaned, "Oh God! I knew I was over there for something, Is Carlton OK?" That was the end of Joe's babysitting but not Joe's friendship.

Maureen, a woman who taught with me in Crestline had three lovely daughters and thought she knew all there was to know about raising and teaching children. During one of her visits to our house, she decided to show us how to teach Carlton to talk. It didn't matter to her that he had never said a word in his life. She was a teacher and teachers taught. Carlton was to look at her, watch her lips and, bingo, he'd never shut up again.

Instead of watching her lips, Carlton grabbed a handful of her hair and almost took her head off. To teach him that pulling hair was a "no, no," she gave his hair a yank. Carlton was upset by this turn of events. He let go of her hair and hid behind the couch. Maureen said that now he was ready to learn. He might have been, but not from her. He stayed behind the couch until she left. From then on, whenever she looked at him, he disappeared behind the couch or under a chair. Carlton never did give her a chance to try out her teaching techniques. He remained content in his silent world.

Carlton invented his own game of hide and seek. He did the hiding and we did the seeking. When Carlton got lost, he had to be found. He didn't vanish often, but when he did it was a neighborhood event. We'd search for him in the house and around the house. The most difficult searches took place when he disappeared while playing outdoors. We knew he couldn't go very far, but he could find his way into small places and under unassuming things. We looked under houses and porches. We looked behind bushes and woodpiles. We searched inside garages and storage sheds. Carlton never hid in the same place twice.

Fortunately for the seekers, once Carlton got where he was going, he made happy gurgling noises. One time the gurgling came from inside our neighbor's dog house. Another time it emanated from under a cardboard box and another from behind a fallen oak. On other occasions the gurgles came from a kitchen cabinet, a closet and once from inside our washing machine. In time he called us to his favorite places and we knew where to go whenever he went missing.

Carlton was double jointed. He could touch his feet together behind his neck. He was able to scratch his ears with his toes. His double jointedness helped him hide in small places. Being double jointed made him a folk hero in our family. His cousins, sisters and brother put on plays and great talent shows every time the family was together. The last act was always Carlton doing his double jointed routine. Everyone gazed in wonder at his contortions. When the curtain fell, there would be thunderous applause. Carlton could hold his own with the best his cousins, sisters and brother had to offer.

Carlton's high pain tolerance presented a grave concern. Nobody knew when he was hurt because he didn't cry until about five minutes after what happened that hurt him. We couldn't tell what was bothering him until we searched his body for injuries. One day after changing Carlton I placed him in his playpen. After a few minutes, he started to cry. I checked his arms, legs and head but found nothing that would cause him distress. I undressed him and to my horror, I discovered that I had pinned his diaper to him. When I saw what I had done I removed the pin, cleaned the wound and then carefully put his diaper back on. This time I made sure that only the diaper had a pin through it.

Carlton once stepped on the grate of our gas floor heater and walked away as if nothing had happened. A little while later he began to whimper, which led me to discover the burn on the sole of his foot. In time we knew he was hurt when he limped or when he cried for no apparent reason. Carlton taught us to be perceptive parents.

OH LITTLE TOWN OF CRESTLINE

Crestline California just about how it looked when we arrived

If your first child was going to be born a mongoloid, Crestline was a great little town to bring him home to. It was surrounded by small communities whose names were conducive to raising a child that needed a quiet, laid back, no questions asked, small town atmosphere. Towns, whose names were soothing to the soul, names like Valley of Enchantment, Cedar Pines Park, Cedar Glen, Valley of the Moon, Skyland, Horseshoe Bend, Arrowhead Highlands and right near our cabin, Inspiration Point. There was no hurry there. The motto of mountain people was, "We don't give a damn what they do down the hill."

Crestline is a small community located in the San Bernardino Mountains about fifteen miles above the city of San Bernardino. It is, at best, a bedroom community to the many towns in the inland empire. In summer it is home to many visitors and second home owners who come to enjoy the mountains and swim and fish in Lake Gregory.

Crestline was a world unto itself. Everyone knew what everyone else was doing and no one seemed to worry too much about it. If someone ran off with someone else's wife, everybody knew about it. If there was an affair going on it was public knowledge It seemed to be the mentality of the town that this is just the way things were. This was life. It was a great place for kids, however, as the woods were their backyard. If all else failed they could go out and hug a tree or watch animals and generally stay out of trouble.

Mimi and I began teaching in Crestline in the late nineteen fifties. At the time it had one small grocery store, a couple of gas stations, numerous bars, a few diner type restaurants, a hardware store, one doctor, no dentist, no bank and very few professional people living there. The townspeople looked up to teachers with their college educations and steady jobs. Teachers were the pillars of the community. Mimi and I knew most of the people living in Crestline, because we taught their children. It was a wonderful place to teach. We had the support of the parents and a support of administration. For a teacher the situation was ideal.

Sometimes a child would do something strange but it didn't bother anyone. A little boy brought a box of kittens to show-and-tell one day. He began his sharing by asking if anyone wanted a cat. One boy told his teacher he decided to have a quick lunch so he ate his quarter. One mother whose son I held back a grade complemented me for being her son's first teacher that didn't get pregnant.

The town was populated with unforgettable characters, the kind of people that made living and working there memorable. Every year the locals took over the Barn. The Barn was just that, a large old barn that had been refurbished into a spacious bar and suspect restaurant. For two weeks each year the Barn became a theatre that was home to the colorful Crashline Players. A local mechanic named Ace played a song on a pair of spoons; three fat performers painted their bellies with eyes, nose and mouth and danced their way to local fame; the chorus line came in all shapes and sizes and very little talent; locals sang, put on skits and made general fools of themselves. This unbelievable production was Crestline at its best. The Barn is now a church, a church with a rich past.

On one occasion, one of the local women who was a little slow showed up pregnant at one of the bars. When she was asked to describe the child's father, she couldn't remember what he looked like or the color of his hair because he hadn't taken his hat off. One young fellow shot baskets at the school and kept track of every basket he ever made. When I moved off the mountain, he was well over nine thousand. When I went back to visit the same young man was into counting the fish he caught. His victims were the crappie that he could catch with cheese as bait. At last count he was well over three thousand. Today he'd be in a special school. In Crestline he was an accepted part of the community.

Ace, the spoon player of the Crashline Players, and his brother Walt owned the local garage at the top of the hill. Ace was quite the lover. When he met a woman at a bar, he would show her a card that verified that he'd had a vasectomy. One of Ace's girlfriend's husbands took offense to Ace's dallying and shot him one afternoon. Ace died on the spot. The Crashline players went on mournfully that night without Ace and his spoons. After the show the cast got together in a different bar to celebrate another successful run of the Crashline. Before the celebration began in earnest, the piano player and one of the singers asked the crowd for a moment of silence for their fallen friend Ace. After the silence the piano began to slowly play and the singer reverently began to sing, "That Old Ace Down In The Hole."

Woody was another character who could only survive on the mountain. . He lived out in an apple orchard with his wife and six kids. He drank too much and did strange things when he'd had a few too many. Once he bet a bar crowd that he had a live rattlesnake underneath his shirt. After all bets were in, he lifted his shirt and sure enough he was hiding a three and a half foot rattler with its mouth taped shut. Woody frequented a bar that had a tree growing right through the roof. The tree separated one corner from the rest of the bar. One night Woody was sitting in that corner talking to a friend around the tree. After a while he excused himself, went out to his truck, got a chain saw, came back and cut the tree down. He said he was tired of having that tree interrupting his conversations. Driving home one night, Woody missed a turn and drove his truck into Lake Gregory. He managed to get out of his truck and make it to land. When he looked back he saw he had forgotten to turn off his lights. He dove back in as he didn't want to mess up his battery.

Yes, Crestline was a wonderful place for Carlton, he fit right in.

The most colorful character, who lived in Crestline, was Mary Tone. She became our dearest friend and our son Tommy's godmother.

MARY SETS THE TONE

Mary Tone greeting students soon after the school was named for her.

When I moved to Crestline I was in for a surprise or two. The first surprise was the beauty of the place, a mountain of rock, filled with cedars, pine trees, blue jays and squirrels. The second surprise came in the form of a mountain of flesh. It was a woman, a most remarkable woman. Over time I came to learn that she needed a large body to contain the extra large heart she hauled around inside of her.

Her name was Mary Tone. She had the cherubic face of one of Michalango's little disembodied angels that flutter about the domes of Rome. When people first saw her they were surprised by her sheer volume, but once they glanced at her beaming face and they unconsciously forgot about the width and depth of the body that pranced around beneath it. At five foot two, she was a one hundred and ninety pound whirlwind. Mary never walked, she galloped. Mary was always in motion. She seemed to be in all places at the same time. Just turn a corner, especially a corner where someone needed help and there was Mary. There wasn't a person on the mountain who didn't smile and wave when she passed by.

Mary was an unforgettable character. She was the kindergarten teacher and volunteer social service agency for the mountain area. Her favorite color was purple. All her clothes were purple, her house was purple and all the furniture in her classroom was painted purple.

Mary had been a riveter during the war. When the war ended she went to college and became a teacher. She moved to Crestline and took over the town with her lust for life. Everyone on the mountain knew and loved Mary Tone. She enjoyed a good party. If there was a band playing at one of the local bars, she would invite them over after hours for a party at her house. Many times things were booming at Mary's house well past four in the morning.

Mary was married once. On her honeymoon she rejected the whole concept of wedded bliss, got off the train and returned to her comfort zone in Crestline. One year she entered the Miss Crestline beauty pageant. She won hands down. Her prize, beside a bouquet of flowers and a trophy with a statue of a thin beauty, was a trip to Las Vegas and the regional beauty finals. When this plump little fortyish elf of a contestant took the stage in her purple long johns, the auditorium went wild. She was the hit of the pageant even though she didn't make it to Atlantic City where she could have become Miss America.

The first time my wife met Mary was at teacher orientation. This funny little lady invited Mimi to lunch. They went to a local restaurant in Lake Arrowhead where Mary ordered Sauerkraut and Champaign. Mimi knew right then that she had met a very special person. She invited us to her house a short time later and we were overcome with the chaos that greeted us in the form of boxes on top of boxes stacked against the walls. She walked along an aisle of boxes, stopped, picked one out of the stack and showed us a hat she had bought four years earlier in Santa Barbara. Her VW van resembled her house. You had to be careful when you opened the door or the social service agency goods would tumble out and smother you. If they didn't crush you her dog, Major might. Major lived in a burrow deep inside the van somewhere. Mary introduced us to many unexpected characters. The Pig Lady who lived in an abandoned mine down in the desert and had the biggest pig I had ever seen. How Mary found her I'll never know. Mary brought her clothes and food each week as one of her extraordinary good deeds. She was also a mother figure for a group of young marines who came up to Crestline, drove her around in an old red Model A Ford and partied all the time.

Mary in Santa Barbara wearing one of her hats

Mary's classroom was nothing but unique. Anything that moved within its walls was dressed in purple. If it didn't move it was painted purple. The children loved Mary Tone. Any child fortunate enough to have her as their kindergarten teacher got off to a fine start. The rewards she gave were in a class of their own. For good citizenship your child might come home with a live guinea pig, a mangled toy, a used tee shirt or, in my own daughter's case, a doll that had melted in a fire and looked like it had cancer. Try as we might we were unable to separate our five year old from that disfigured prize.

On one occasion Mary let the children handle a small king snake. At the end of the day the snake had disappeared. Mary and the children were upset at the loss of their pet. Mary got a call that night from an irate but understanding parent who had found the lost snake in her daughter's underwear when she was getting her ready for bed. Mary and the class were elated that nothing terrible had happened to their friend, the snake.

In order to get college credits to move up on the pay scale teachers had to take college courses. One time many of us decided to take Spanish together. The only thing Mary could grasp was the word "la". From that time on, feeling she had mastered the Spanish language and become bilingual, she used it on a daily basis. "La shoe, la school, la car, la snake." La became part of her daily speech.

Mary had a special place in her heart for Carlton. From the day he was born she checked on his wellbeing every chance she had. As the informal social service agency for the mountain, Mary would collect clothes, shoes, blankets and anything else that the less fortunate mountaineers might find useful. There were a lot of families that were barely making it in the Crestline community. As our family grew we contributed the clothes and shoes our children had outgrown to Mary, knowing they would be put to good use. Every once in a while Mary put our family in that needy group, probably because of Carlton, whom she dearly loved. She would bring nice clothes and shoes for our kids. Invariably they were the same clothes and shoes we had given her some weeks prior.

After living in Crestline for ten wonderful years, it was a time for a change. I received a fellowship to Syracuse University where we were going to be living for a year. Carlton had been out of our home for the past few months and was at the time in Pacific State hospital and would be there for a year until we returned and were a complete family again. We packed up the Dodge Van and headed toward New York for a year of study. We arranged for student housing and enrolled our children in the local elementary school. Colleen was entering second grade and Tommy, Mary's Godson, would be going into first. When we presented our children to the principal, he looked at their report cards and asked who the Golden Horse was. Unbeknownst to us, Mary had signed all the kindergarten report cards as the "Golden Horse." One day Mary had attended a funeral of a friend. Instead of her usual purple, she returned to her classroom looking radiant in a sparkly gold and white suit. Upon seeing her, one of her five year old students saw her and yelled out "Miss Tone you look like a golden horse". From that day on Mary Tone considered herself a golden horse.

Mary died in Crestline some thirty years ago. The town hasn't changed much, though few people living there can remember Mary Tone. The town will, however, have a landmark to remember her by. Upon Mary's death the town named the Elementary School after her. After much debate it became the Mary Tone School instead of Golden Horse Academy.

Carlton was Mary's special friend. Every time Mary would come to visit, he would light up and let it be known by his high spirited quacks that his Mary was there. I don't think Mary even thought he was retarded; he was just another child who, like all children, was special to Mary. And to Carlton Mary Tone was always his very own Golden Horse.

One of Mary's infamous Christmas Cards. Yes, the Golden Horse is on the Golden Throne. Even her bathroom was crammed with stuff.

A CHRISTMAS STORY

The Christmas season with all its frills is special to the Smith Family because Mimi and I come from families whose traditions are the end result of generations of Christmas fanatics.

My own father and mother use to decorate the whole house along with a huge tree on Christmas Eve while I was sleeping. They gave Santa Claus all the credit. Today, when we decorate our own tree, I wonder how they did it. The tree was enormous and the decorations too numerous to count. The manger scene was elaborate; complete with my Dad's little "Bethlehem City Limits." roadside sign. Christmas morning they'd get me dressed and rush me off to church before I could see the wonders that Santa had managed on Christmas Eve. When I returned home I was escorted into the glorious Christmas Room with its beautiful tree and gifts galore. It was a magical day.

Mimi's mom and dad started the Christmas season by purchasing the perfect tree. Perfect at least in the eyes of Mimi's mother. Some years her dad had to buy two or three trees and bring each one home before her mother was satisfied and it was decorated with the family ornaments. Christmas day meant church, gifts and a scrumptious family meal, two or three kinds of meat, vegetables and desserts baked by a mother who loved to cook. Santa got all the credit from Mimi, her sister and two brothers.

On our first Christmas, Mimi and I were living in the old schoolhouse in the San Bernardino Mountains. Mimi was pregnant with Carlton. We were struggling to keep ahead of the bill collectors, but it was Christmas and we were from Christmas families so we carried on our tradition.

My job as an outdoor education teacher consisted of taking sixth graders on a series of nature hikes in the forest. On these hikes I kept my eye out for the perfect Christmas tree. When I found it I marked it in my memory for the night when I would hike out to it, ax in hand, chop it down and bring it home to my adoring wife.

When the time came, I went proudly into the woods to the tree that would inaugurate our own Christmas tradition. I must have hiked a mile to get to my tree. I cut it down and carried it home triumphantly; joyful to be providing the centerpiece for our Christmas celebration and relieved that no one caught me chopping down a live tree in a national forest. When I got home Mimi asked me "What is that thing?" I explained that it was the beautiful tree I had told her about. She said it looked more like a weed than a tree. I was crushed. I stood the tree up to its full three foot height and tried desperately to get her approval. I explained that we could put it on a table and that it would be perfect. With tears in her eyes and a promise that this would be our last three foot tree, she consented. We decorated our tree with one string of lights, a few ornaments, a string of popcorn and some tinsel.

That was our last Christmas alone for the next thirty years and our last dinky tree. The string of lights from our first tree lasted for many years. We still hang those original ornaments each year. We always string popcorn and tinsel as we did on our first Christmas together. It's become our tradition.

Christmas was always a production for our family. I went out and cut two large, full trees, one for my friend who owned the woods and one for me. I hauled my tree home. After trimming about three feet off the bottom each year, I put what was left in front of our living room window. Mimi and I decorated it with strings of popcorn and garlands of cranberries. I put the tinsel on strand by strand. After we finished decorating the tree we spread sheets underneath it. We then added the finishing touch, a picket fence around the outside to protect it from Carlton, Colleen and Tommy. Every once in a while the fence was breached and low lying popcorn and cranberries disappeared along with candy canes and chocolate ornaments.

Carlton eating some popcorn off the tree about 7 years old

Each year at Christmas we took a shopping trip to White Front so the kids could have their pictures taken with Santa Claus. One year before Alicia was born we bundled Carlton, Colleen and Tommy into our VW Bug and headed for our annual picture with Santa. We envisioned their joyful faces, beaming with great expectations as they looked into the eyes of this most jolly gentleman. Colleen leaped into his lap and recited a litany of wants. She was enthralled with the possibility that by merely telling him, her wants would come true. When it was Tommy's turn, he took one look at the old white bearded face. He figured no present was worth this, let out a scream and fled to his mother's arms. It seemed Santa had had a long day and wasn't ready when Carlton was placed on his lap. Before he was able to say "HO, HO, HO" Carlton grabbed his beard. By the time we got the beard out of Carlton's left hand, he had Santa's hat in his right. All the time Santa was saying through clenched teeth "and what do you want for Christmas young man?" Carlton was saying "UH, UH, UH" and not letting go of anything. Finally Mimi and I rescued Santa. We thanked him for his patience and were given a memorable photo of a happy Carlton with a disheveled, confused St. Nick.

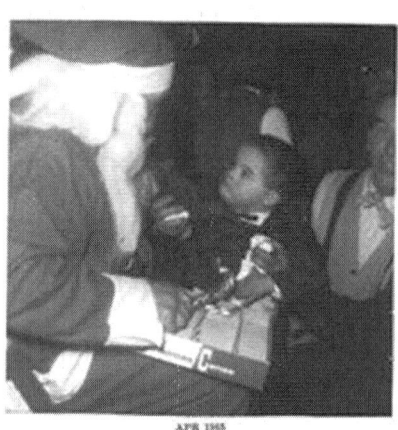

Carlton confusing Santa

One of our best Santa Claus visits was the year Santa came to our church in Crestline. Santa was a friend of ours. After consulting with Mimi and I, Santa told the kids what they had to do if they wanted him to visit the house, bag in hand, on Christmas night. Colleen was to help her mother and go to bed when she was told. Tommy was told to stop having accidents in his pants. He was under so much pressure to achieve this goal that we had our hands full getting him off the pot for the rest of the Christmas holiday. Carlton sat docily in Santa's lap while I held his hands behind his back.

As the years passed and our family grew with the birth of Alicia, the Christmas Eve tree decorating tradition became a family decorating party well before Christmas day. Our visits to Santa Claus continued. When Colleen and Tommy reached the age of doubt but not quite the age of dis- belief, they went along so Alicia would get the full benefit of visiting this magical person. In time she too found it unnecessary to sit on the lap of the jolly white bearded fellow in the red suit. One of our Christmas traditions had come to an end

Throughout the years our trees remained tall and full. We decorated them with strings of popcorn and cranberries. We placed tinsel on the tree one strand at a time. The accumulation of ornaments filled every nook and cranny and we strung enough lights on the tree to light a baseball stadium.

The picket fence disappeared, but the spirit of Christmas was always with us as was Carlton who was home for Christmas for as long as he lived.

THIEF OF DREAMS

Bandit

Our friends the Goodwins had an English bulldog named Max, a big, wavy jowled, mutt that resembled Winston Churchill and was slow, uncoordinated, always dirty and had bad breath. He couldn't do much more than drag his stomach along the ground and let the neighborhood kids swing him in a hammock. Why I was attracted to him, I'll never know.

Beyond all odds, this unattractive canine became pregnant. That's when the Goodwins discovered that Max was a Maxine. My attraction to Max proved to be a fatal attraction. Even though I saw her as a hopeless mutt, I still wanted to take one of her pups. The puppy I chose was destined to modify our love for dogs for the rest of our lives.

When Max had her litter, Mimi and I were living in our small cabin at the camp where I was teaching. Mimi was five months pregnant with

Carlton. We felt that by the time the baby was born, we'd have our puppy trained and ready to protect us from harm. We also wanted our child to grow up loving animals.

I was the only person they could find who wanted any of the puppies so the Goodwins gave me the pick of the litter. I was attracted to a white pup with a black patch over its right eye. He looked like your run of the mill burglar so we called him Bandit.

Bandit moved into our humble abode early in February. He was a feisty little guy, playful, wild, cute as only a puppy can be, mischievous, always under foot and capable of eating anything. Bandit could also yodel at any time of the day or night. Between Carlton who was born in April and Bandit, our life was full.

From the start, there was no love lost between Bandit and Mimi. Every time I left the house, he'd go into hysterics. He'd whine or cry until I returned and sometimes it would carry on for three or four hours. Whenever Mimi left, he'd wag his tail and lie down contentedly in a corner of the room. When Mimi hung clothes on the clothesline, Bandit would eat her clothes and leave mine alone. He'd eat her slippers, hide her shoes and chew her sweaters.

When Mimi was eight and a half months pregnant, Bandit stole her stockings. He did his puppy dance and ducked under the bed. Mimi gave chase; she was sick and tired of being taken advantage of by an ungrateful canine. She went under the bed after him. He backed further into a corner just out of her reach. Mimi tried to get to him but she could go no farther. She couldn't go backward either. She was stuck. Bandit left his hideout and began to whine. He was upset with her for not playing anymore. When I got home I lifted the bed and simultaneously freed my wife and restrained her from killing our dog.

We began to notice that lots of household items, dishes, tools, socks, silverware and books were disappearing, including Carlton's bottles. Occasionally loose change seemed to be roll out of our lives. Mimi and I talked it over and decided that the thief was either, one of us, Carlton or Bandit. She said it wasn't her. I said it wasn't me. Carlton was four weeks old so we had good idea it wasn't him. That left Bandit.

We decided to set up a surveillance system. Two hours on, two hours off for Mimi and me. We were determined to watch him day and night. We left bait around; a screw driver, an electric saw, a sock, a wooden spoon, a toy and an empty baby bottle. He took them all to a hiding place under the house.

We recovered everything that he couldn't eat. Discovering his hideout made life a little easier. Now when something disappeared we knew where to could find it.

One morning Mimi was feeding Carlton. As she was cuddling her son, she reached for her wedding and engagement rings as she had taken them off to clean them. When she cleaned her rings, she put them on the edge of our bed. They weren't there. She searched the house but they were nowhere to be found. She was frantic.

When I arrived home for lunch she blurted out the upsetting news. I searched, she searched, and then we both looked at Bandit. He was wagging his tail, yapping and thoroughly enjoying all the excitement. Mimi looked at me and gasped "he wouldn't". I wasn't sure whether he would or wouldn't, but I was pretty sure that he might.

There was a big pine tree in front of our cabin. I attached Bandit to that tree with ten foot rope. I explained to Mimi, "what goes in must come out." Bandit wasn't about to set foot in our house until Mimi's ring reappeared and was back on her finger. We waited. Each time Bandit had a bowel movement, I was right on top of it with a long stick. The following morning after three negative probes I hit pay dirt. My stick struck metal in an extra large mound. The thrill of discovery overwhelmed me.

Finding the rings was just the beginning. Extracting and cleaning our treasure still lie ahead. I got a clothes hanger and was able to spear both rings. I gingerly took them to a water faucet, turned the water on full blast and washed them. We took them into the cabin where, with the aid of every modern cleaning chemical, Mimi got them back to mint condition. Bandit was freed from his ten foot encampment. Things would never be the same, however, for the bond of trust that exists between a man and his dog was forever shaken.

I was a teacher in an Outdoor Education program in Crestline. Every sixth grade child from Norwalk and La Mirada spent a school week at camp studying nature and the environment. Our camp was a showplace. We had visitors from all over the world come to see how schools could use camping as an important curriculum tool. It was part of my job to show them around and explain the program.

One day after a night of rain, we had a group of visitors from Pakistan. It just so happened that Mimi had decided to take Carlton for a morning stroll through the camp that day. She often took walks to get away from our small cabin and from our dog. As she was approaching our group, a muddy mess came roaring towards us. Mimi moved out of the way as Bandit hurled himself on one of our visitors. His muddy paws landed on the gentlemen's shoulders and worked their way down the front of his powder blue suit. Bandit was smothering our visitor with puppy love.

I immediately asked anyone who was within earshot "whose dog is that?" The only person around was Mimi. She was shaking her head as if she'd never seen him before. All the while Bandit was jumping around Mimi and Carlton, wagging his tail. Mimi pretended she didn't even know who that dog was or why he was attracted to her. She kept saying "shoo shoo!" Bandit just jumped higher, then went off chasing squirrels.

I apologized to our visitor and assured him that whoever owned that mutt would be chastised. He accepted my apology with a bow and continued the tour a lot worse for wear. I knew I had to do something about that pup but I didn't know what.

That summer we bought a house closer to town. It was surrounded by lots of land, a place for our dog to roam freely. We pictured Bandit cruising the property, protecting us from intruders, fetching the newspaper and being man's best friend and faithful servant.

The thrill of ownership glowed within us as we painted bedrooms and decorated walls. It was the best of times. There were no leash laws on the mountain so Bandit was free to chase birds and squirrels. Our neighbors down the hill from us were a Swiss couple, Moritz and Lena Boll. Flowers of every kind and color shown like a rainbow in their meticulously ordered garden.

One day Moritz came up to see me while I was weeding my paltry patch of native plants. He asked me if Bandit was my pooch. When I proudly admitted to the ownership of said pooch, Moritz looked at me as only a Swiss patriarch can and said "I shot the last pooch that lived here". I assured Moritz that Bandit would never again leave our unfenced property and then proceeded to look for a nice spot to bury Bandit after Moritz shot him. From that day on, Moritz and Lena brought delicious bones for Bandit. But they always snuck around the block and delivered them to our front door so Bandit wouldn't see where the bones came from. Bandit never would stay on our property but he never set foot on their property the whole time he was with us. Bandit was not a dumb dog. He loved his bones and knew where they were coming from.

We fed Bandit. Moritz and Lena fed Bandit but Bandit was never satisfied. He had an insatiable appetite. One morning, when Mimi went to feed him, he was no where to be found. Not only was Bandit missing, but his food pan was gone too. Could he have been dognapped? No such luck. Mimi looked up the road and there, carrying his food pan in his mouth, was Bandit. He was going from house to house begging for food. He made begging a part of his daily routine.

When he wasn't eating or begging, Bandit was out in the neighborhood destroying kids' shirts and jackets. In his playful way he would bite a shirt tail or jacket flap and run home to share his prize with us. Often he was followed by a child and an irate parent seeking recompense.

Being a teacher in a small town didn't help matters. Everyone knew me and my dog. Every torn shirt and jacket found its way to my house or to my classroom. It made no difference whether Bandit had eaten it or not. He was guilty by association. It was embarrassing and humiliating for Mimi and me. Bandit was eating us out of house and home and now he was costing us a fortune in clothing replacement.

I finally figured that freedom was not what Bandit needed most, so I tethered him to a tree. I gave him plenty of rope, enough to hang himself. However he was not a dog to be tied up or hanged. Instead he chewed through the rope and went merrily on his way, begging and eating clothing. The only difference being that now he was dragging a long rope behind him.

Winter in the mountain was cold and damp. It either rained or snowed. We couldn't leave Bandit outside. Mimi and I enjoyed our winter evenings in front of a warming fire. I had this dream of the Smiths as a perfect family, I, in my reclining chair, smoking my pipe, reading my newspaper, faithful dog at my side, Mimi, reading her book or doing embroidery or playing with Carlton. Occasionally we'd share small tidbits of information we knew would interest the other. Reality never seemed to match our dreams. I did read the newspaper once in a while and Mimi sometimes played with Carlton or read a book. I never did smoke a pipe, own a reclining chair or have a faithful dog.

Bandit was the reason we couldn't enjoy this dream. Every night he would lie on our braided rug in front of the fire and let off gas. Whatever he was getting in that food pan was leaving him painfully full of gas. He'd lay there sighing and farting. The horrible odor permeated the house. We were forced to take refuge in the breakfast nook or our bedroom, while Bandit just lay there stinking up our world.

We were beside ourselves. I tried putting him outside between bursts, but that didn't work. I was never able to time things. I was either a little too early or a little too late. Even if he did let one go outside he'd save enough to asphyxiate us when he came back in. Worse yet, while we were exiled to the dining nook, he ate a hole in our braided rug. We ended up with no fire in the fire place, Bandit in the living room, Mimi, Carlton and I in the bedroom or breakfast nook, no pipe, no easy chair, a hole in our good rug and nothing to share but the smell of Bandit.

During the day I tied him to his tree. Each day he chewed through his rope and came to visit me at school. I brought him home and doubled the rope. It finally dawned on me that rope alone would never restrain an escape artist of this magnitude so I bought a chain and chained him to his tree. I figured, if he was chained to a tree he wouldn't get himself shot, go begging, eat jackets or follow me to school. I wasn't too worried about the gas because he was outside. This worked fine for the first two days. On the third day he showed up at school chain and all. I figured he had probably eaten the tree. I'd had it. I took him back home and told Mimi that the next time he came to see me, he'd be gone. I was going to have Animal Control find him a new home

The inevitable happened the very next day. I was teaching my sixth graders when Bandit, chain and all, appeared at the door of my classroom. My classroom was in a small out building that had a fence all around it. I stuck Bandit in the back yard and called Animal Control at my first opportunity. I told them a stray dog was bothering the educational processes of our mountain youth. They told me they would be in the area shortly and would pick up the stray.

They arrived just after noon. I led them to the stray dog in my schoolyard. They grabbed the chain and were leading him away when Mary Tone, the kindergarten teacher and animal lover came running out of her room yelling, "Stop! That dog belongs to Carl Smith." I said to her "Mary, it only looks like my dog, it has no license so it couldn't be mine." Being an animal lover, Mary couldn't bare to see any dog go to the pound. She didn't fall down in front of the dog catcher's truck but she came close. I convinced her that the dog was a threat to the children, the school, the town and to society in general. She wasn't convinced, but she finally let them take Bandit.

I had mixed emotions as they took him away. There were many things about him that I would miss. Then again I felt a great deal of relief.

When I got home from school that afternoon I told Mimi of our good fortune. Of course we both had some regrets. Bandit had influenced our lives. We knew that we'd probably never have another dog again because Bandit had stolen our hearts along with our sanity. As we sat in front of a roaring fire that night, Mimi looked up from her book and expressed her hope that Bandit would find a nice new home with plenty of kids, a fenced in yard, lots of food, clothes to eat and a family with a congenital disease that caused them to lose their sense of smell.

MARY ALICE

My mom Mary Alice with Carlton when he was about 7 years old

Thinking about my mother reminds me of a song we sing in church:

GENTLE WOMAN---------QUIET LIGHT
MORNING STAR---------SO STRONG AND BRIGHT

Mary Alice, my mother was a small woman, four foot ten, gentle, patient and non- judgmental. She helped Mimi and me through some very trying times. Her love for Carlton made it possible for us to raise our family in a fairly normal way.

Mary Alice lived in the time before computers. In the early years of her marriage to my father her life was filled with excitement. My dad was writing vaudeville acts and Broadway plays and working with Ziegfeld writing for the Follies. It was the 1920s and life was roaring. My mom was part of the Broadway crowd. She loved it. If she could, she would have loved to live in downtown Manhattan all her life.

When she and dad moved to Hollywood in 1930, life was still good but it was no Broadway. She was separated from friends and family and busy raising four children. She compensated for this new life by writing weekly letters to her family. When her children, my brother and two sisters and I grew up and went our own way, the weekly letters kept coming. Being the youngest, I got the last carbon copy of the family newsletter. Her letters were always positive. She relayed the latest news about her family. She wrote about her grandchildren, uncles, aunts, my brother, my sisters and me so we would be aware of what was going on within our whole family. Mary Alice ensured that birthdays were never missed.

Mary Alice had a special place in her heart for Carlton. She never prayed for a cure, she just wanted him to have a happy life. She answered her own prayers. Carlton's life was a happy one because of her. Mary Alice would walk over to our house every day to help Mimi. She would rock and feed Carlton while Mimi boiled bottles and washed diapers. When Carlton was asleep, she'd iron and sort clothes that Mimi had attempted to hide from her so she wouldn't do so much. We never asked her for help, she just provided it. Mimi always said that Mary Alice was the perfect mother-in-law.

When Mary Alice wasn't at our house she was home typing for my father. Dad was a prolific writer who wrote stories and articles for the local paper. He recorded all his writings on a sound scriber. My Mother transcribed them all. My Dad didn't like criticism. My Mother never criticized his work; she just changed what she felt needed changing. Mary Alice most likely attained sainthood just by living with my father. She reminded Dad of every birthday or important milestone in the life of our family. He would create a special card for the occasion. While Mom was comforting and rocking Carlton, Dad would create toys in his workshop. The toys were usually noise making contraptions, like a couple of springs with knobs on them attached to pie tins. Carlton could lie in his crib and bang them loudly. Carlton loved the noise. If it wasn't a noisy toy it would be a ball that didn't roll straight or a crooked bat to hit the crazy ball.

Mimi and I wanted my dad to stick to his writing because his toys were driving us nuts. Carlton was the apple of his grandpa's eyes.

Carlton and Mary Alice's relationship was surreal. While she rocked him they seemed to communicate. She knew exactly what he wanted. She knew when he was tired, hungry, thirsty or in need of a change. It was as if they were talking to one another. She was the only person that claimed he could talk. He talked to her.

When Colleen was born, I decided to surprise Mimi by completely remodeling our kitchen. When Mimi and I left for the hospital my friends came over and stripped the kitchen down to its bare walls. All that remained was the sink. We put the refrigerator on the back porch so our food wouldn't spoil. Due to a lack of time and poor coordination, our plans for the big surprise failed to materialize, so Mimi and her new baby had to stay at a friend's house for a week while we finished the job. My mother came over every day to take care of Carlton while I was teaching school. Cold bottles, cold sandwiches, baths in the sink and fruit kept us alive until Mimi could return to her almost remodeled kitchen. Two months later the tile work was finally completed.

Not long after the kitchen fiasco, Mimi found herself pregnant again. Our son Tom was born on December 26, 1961, eleven months to the day after his sister Colleen's birth. Two babies in the same year, "Irish twins". In order to celebrate Tom's birth I had to surprise Mimi with yet another home improvement project. The lone bathroom in our house was inadequate, especially with three babies in diapers, so I decided to surprise Mimi with a new bathroom. When I told mom about my plans for the new bathroom, she understandingly said "that would be nice", gentle soul that she was. This time I used my head and informed Mimi of my magnificent plan. She gave the green light it as long as there was a working toilet when she got home. The bathroom would still be incomplete today if Mary Alice had not been around to mother Carlton and Colleen. She managed to keep the kids fed, bathed and out of our way while keeping the house clean, with the only one available working sink in the kitchen.

My friend Hal Perry came over and helped me tear everything out of the bathroom. When Mimi got home with Tom she had a brand new closet in our bedroom and a toilet in a room with a large hole in the floor where a bathtub and two new sinks should have been. Standing in the hole she found my friend Hal who assured her that we were almost done.

Mom was delighted to see her new grandson Tom and was seemingly unmoved by the disaster that Mimi had come home to. In time, the bathroom was completed with two sinks and a beautiful blue bathtub. Life became much easier for our growing family.

A year or so later, when Mimi came down with diabetes, Mary Alice was there to calm the storm. None of us knew what was happening at the time. Mimi was thirsty all the time, losing weight and losing patience. Mom came over every day to see that Mimi got some rest. She took care of the babies and kept the house and laundry under control as Mimi was nearly incapacitated. After a diagnosis of Type I diabetes and a stay in the hospital, Mimi was able to stabilize her blood sugar. Mary Alice made it possible for her to keep on schedule by being there to help with the kids.

Mary Alice never complained; she always did what needed to be done. All this time she typed and edited dad's stories, wrote family letters and enjoyed her other grandchildren.

Our daughter Alicia was born in 1965. Mary Alice was there again, quietly keeping things under control. By now Colleen and Tom were passing Carlton up both physically and mentally. With a new baby thrown into the mix and diabetes keeping Mimi busy, weighing food and managing her blood sugar, mother was there almost unseen, playing with the kids, rocking Carlton, washing clothes, helping Mimi in the kitchen and letting Mimi and I have a life. To this day I don't know how that little lady did it.

In 1967 mom and dad moved to San Diego. They left a tremendous void. We soon realized how much Mary Alice had done for our family. Without her help our lives would have been very different. She had seen us through some very difficult times and made the early years of our marriage manageable. She was a huge part of our children's lives.

Our family had planned to move to Syracuse, New York soon after my mom and dad moved to San Diego. I had received a fellowship for a year's study at Syracuse University. Many things happened the months before we were to make the move to Syracuse. Mimi was trying to keep her diabetes under control. Carlton's brother and sisters were passing him up physically and mentally.

We had discussed placing Carlton in Pacific State Hospital, but we could not bring ourselves to do it. One day we got a call from our Social Worker about a brand new facility for severely handicapped persons that was opening in Bloomington, not too far from Crestline. We visited and felt it might be a good place for Carlton. After much soul searching we decided to let go of our son and trust his care to others. The new facility proved to be a bust after a few months so we had no choice but to place Carlton in Pacific State Hospital.

In San Diego, my mom's and dad's health was beginning to fail and then my father died. We were torn. Should we go or should we stay to be with my mom? Mary Alice insisted that we go and promised to be there when we came back.

The day we left for Syracuse we visited Carlton at Pacific State Hospital. The conditions at Pacific were so bad that we worried we might never see him again. While we were in Syracuse the State of California was in the process trying to place children like Carlton back into the community in small homes. Fortunately for Carlton and our family Carlton was placed in the home of a wonderful woman named Gladys Belleheumer. We kept in contact with her and related Carlton's progress to Mary Alice, who was living in a small house in San Diego that the family had owned since 1918.

Mom had come down with cancer and like everything else she accepted her cancer as just another part of life. Her weekly letters kept us posted on the comings and goings of all the family. She kept busy walking to the market and taking the bus to the cancer clinic for treatment.

One day Mrs. Belleheumer brought Carlton down to see his grandmother. Shortly after the visit my mom sent us a long letter describing the Belleheumers and Carlton. She told us about her visit with the Belleheumers and their boys. She also managed to relay in her letter how inadequate she was as a hostess. The Belleheumers stayed two and a half hours longer than they had anticipated and in a long letter raved about the visit and the gracious hostess that welcomed them and their boys.

Mary Alice stayed alive until we came home from Syracuse. Her health was failing but she kept her promise to be there when we returned. She passed away four weeks after our return. During those four weeks she talked to Mimi about her life and the exciting times she had in New York and Hollywood. She told Mimi that as exciting as those days were, they didn't hold a candle to the time she spent with Carlton.

The dearest person in his life was his grandmother, Mary Alice. Their favorite activity was to sit in our rocking chair and rock for hours on end. Every gentle movement of that chair revealed the love that existed between the two. After Mary Alice passed away Carlton still loved to rock. When he did he must have felt he was back in the arms of the person he loved the most, in a place he loved to be, doing the thing he love most to do.

When I think back over the early years of our marriage, I realize that gentle Mary Alice played a saintly role. She helped Mimi and me through the most difficult years of our lives. She was a rock. Everything she did for us and for her grandchildren she did with unconditional love. She was the perfect grandmother. She stayed alive to see and enjoy her Colleen, Tommy, Alicia and the love of her life, Carlton. It saddens me that Mary Alice didn't live long enough for her grandkids to really get to know her the only one that knew his grandma was Carlton. He even had conversations with her.

GENTLE WOMAN--------PEACEFUL DOVE
TEACH ME WISDOM-------TEACH ME LOVE

GREAT AUNT DOT

When I first began to write my memories and stories about Carlton and the memories and stories started to form a book this chapter was hotly debated by family, Mimi, and my tough editor (Alicia). The argument was that this chapter did not fit but we came to a mutual agreement that the story of Carlton would be incomplete without Great Aunt Dot and it was alright that the chapter did not fit because Great Aunt Dot herself never fit in. Great Aunt Dot was a deep red rose in a field of white carnations. She stood out. She was the proverbial square peg that could never fit into the round hole that society had dug for woman of her time. Great Aunt Dot was as frightening as she was wonderful and she was the most prolific letter writer of all. Her letters are a study in the attitudes of people toward the developmentally disabled. The letters are also a study in how her personal views changed when Carlton touched her heart. The humor is hard to miss but it is a humor born of distance, experience and time.

My Aunt Dot was a tough old gal with a heart of gold. She is a perfect example of how Carlton enlightened us all and truly opened her eyes to just accept and let it be. In time each and every family member including Dot came to realize that Carlton was perfect in his imperfection.

Dearie and Dot lived way down south in San Diego. In the eyes of a grandson and nephew who lived way up north in Los Angeles they were a wondrous pair. When they came to visit they spoiled me blind. They were my dad's mother and sister, my grandmother Dearie and my aunt Dot. I remember infrequent visits, some by us to San Diego and some by them to Hollywood.

I was still very young when Dearie died, but memories are warm as only memories of grandmas can be. Visits to San Diego, hiking in their beautiful canyon filled with fruit trees, exploring Adams Avenue and eating lavish amounts of goodies were Heaven to an eight year old.

My aunt Dot was different. After Dearie's death, she stayed on in the family estate, which consisted of two small white clapboard houses in Normal Heights. She was a plain looking woman. She always wore what I looked to me to be the same dress. Actually it probably was one of many plain blue dresses from the same Bargain Basement. She was tall for her time, never married and was a woman of many causes.

My dad and his sister were never close. Their father died when my dad was four and Dorothy five. From what my dad told me, they were always competing with each other. During elementary school he skipped a grade. Therefore they both graduated from parochial school in the same class. Today that would be grounds for murder. Back then it seemed to be grounds for life long animosity.

As the years progressed, Dot and her mother moved to the little house in the Normal Heights neighborhood that my dad had bought for them. Dad stayed in Chicago to seek his fortune as an author of vaudeville acts.

Dot became a schoolteacher and eventually the principal of an elementary school. In the early nineteen thirties something happened. Dot's years as an educator came to a screeching halt. No one ever spoke to me about it, but in time, I heard rumors nervous breakdowns, disastrous love affairs and mental illness as possible reasons for her sudden withdrawal from education. Finished with her career in education, she quickly assumed a new role as woman of many causes. She devoted the rest of her life to good works. She went about curing the ills of San Diego. She was a seeker of justice, protector of Balboa Park, leader in the battle for rights of any kind, staunch Democrat and "Good Witch" to all the neighborhood children. Dot was also a prolific writer of letters.

Dot allowed my brother, sisters, and I to visit her one at a time. When my turn came for the annual visit, I was ecstatic. It was my opportunity to be a prince for a week. Dot didn't care for kings but she did love princes. She took me to the zoo, the Cafe Del Rey Moro for lunch and the El Cortez to see the view. We never ate there, we just looked. She even allowed me to play in her Garden-of-Allah like canyon; Dot was the epitome of auntiness.

GREAT AUNT DOT

Writing letters consumed Dot. She wrote letters to editors, movie stars, poets, famous people and my mom. In 1942, my grandmother had an accident and was hospitalized. Dot always had a paranoid way about her. She was the eternal family outcast. In the letter about the accident Dot, living up to form, told Mom about it.

> *Dearie thought of having me wire you when the accident first happened, but I told her nobody up there would care, and she realizes that herself now. We've had an illuminating insight into how we rate with the family. We know now that we've been under a misapprehension all the years, that what we took for affection was just kindness and politeness. Well, thanks for them, anyway. People are lucky who are so rich in friends that they can afford to throw away the oldest and truest"*

When I graduated from eighth grade our relationship began to crumble. My mother answered Dot's weekly letters and let her in on all the comings and goings of her family to the north. In one of her letters Mom told Dot of my impending graduation from eighth grade and Dot sent me the perfect graduation gift, a briefcase. Naturally I was stunned. What should I do with a thing like that? How should I write and thank her for a briefcase? I knew I had to write a thank-you letter or my gentle, loving, sainted mother would kill me. Days went by; I was putting off writing the most epic letter of my life for as long as I could. "As long as I could," arrived in the form of a letter from Dot.

> *"Don't bother thanking me for the briefcase, in fact don't bother me Period!"*

Shortly after that, my grandmother died and Dot wrote Mom another letter.

> *"I'm sure of this: Mother's away on a lovely, joyous vacation, and she knows now that I truly loved her and forgives me my human blunders. My little darling, she was such a kid---sometimes a bad little kid, but she was all mine. She was sort of chum to me. No one will ever love me as she did, in fact, no one will ever care for me at all again in this*

> life. But I know there are other experiences beyond, and other chances, and that we have opportunity to make use of what we've learned here so stumblingly. Mother and I always knew we were misfits. We knew we didn't measure up, and it drew us ever so close. I'm so glad we decided not to have you come down. It would be so completely useless, especially in these days of jammed transportation. Everything was so simple, just one dear friend and I to see her body interred--that little old tired body with its one leg shorter than the other. This little flower was one in a vase in the room when she died, I thought my brother would like to keep it."

From that point in time, we kept in touch mostly through my mom's letters. Without my mother's patience and weekly letters, Dot would probably have given the family houses to some church or organization that she was campaigning for at the time. I still went down to visit her once in awhile but only for an afternoon and more or less as a fallen warrior, not as a prince. If we went out, we'd always go to the Cafe Del Rey Moro, her favorite place to eat in the whole world. Her little pink electric three-wheeled car would be parked in front of her house, plugged into the nearest electrical outlet. Dot was the first and last on the block to own one of these "cars of the future" Her little house was littered with everything she ever owned or read, a veritable treasure chest for nostalgia buffs. I noticed she was very much alone, unknown, even to her neighbors. And her letters kept coming but now they were from a happier Dot. Though still a Dot who seemed to be marching to a different drummer.

> "I've gotten such a thrill out of my Christmas this year. For once the presents I got for everyone were just exactly what I thought would please them best---- no hurry, no rush, no having to take leftovers, and Alice I know you will fix them up like a million dollars--- much better than I could do myself. Wasn't that a good plan of mine to send everybody's present to someone else? Then there's no danger of anyone finding out or even having a chance to speculate on what it might be. I'll be thinking of you on Xmas when the surprise breaks! I wish I could see your faces when my brother opens his. I've been just wondering Al, do you think you could

pick up some special cards to go with each gift? No, that would be too much bother. Never mind."

One time she wrote Mom concerning her needs of the moment.

> *Alice, could I borrow back for a while the hypodermic needle, please? I'm taking injections of tin--- did you ever hear anything so weird? The doctor says I gave a little too much blood to the Red Cross--- I was going to give a gallon but only got up to 7 pints. Don't mention it, please, because it might discourage others from giving and there really is no cause, as he says this wouldn't happen once in thousand times. It isn't serious and is easily curable, but I'll just have to be taking these injections for a while and when I get the needle Tess says she will give them to me, saving me some money and lots of trouble. I'll send it back again when through, for with your big bunch you're more likely to need it than I. We're sure lucky to have it in the family. They are absolutely unobtainable now, and ours is an extra good one----cost ten bucks, the doc says I'll be Ok in six months."*

Poor Mom had to answer these letters because none of the rest of us knew where to begin to unravel the mysteries of this marvelous character

When I was in the Navy and stationed for awhile in San Diego, I'd visit Aunt Dot. The clutter in her little house was more pronounced by this time. During our visits she'd go on about social justice, women's rights, the uselessness of war and all the other things a twenty-one year old sailor wanted to hear about. She always seemed happy that I had stopped by to see her.

When I got out of the Navy, I finished college. I didn't send Dot an announcement of my graduation for fear of reviving memories of an unloved briefcase. In 1958, I met and married the girl of my dreams. As fate would have it, Dot's invitation was the only one that failed to get delivered. A letter from my mom and a picture of the new bride and groom saved the day. Dot was not offended but very happy for her young dethroned prince and his new bride, Mimi.

Soon after we were married I took Mimi to San Diego to meet her new aunt. I knocked on Dot's door. The familiar voice called "Come in." We entered and walked through a maze of boxes of what can only be described as junk. The litter was getting deeper. Before I could introduce Mimi, Dot said, "Listen to this and tell me what you think". She then quoted some obsolete poet and left us both speechless. We went out for lunch at her favorite restaurant, the Cafe Del Rey Moro. The restaurant was in disrepair. The windows were dirty, there were dead flies on the windowsills, and the place was a mess. As Mimi and I gingerly ate our lunch, all Dot could talk about was the beauty of the place. She saw regal surroundings, classy waiters, a jewel in the midst of her sacred Balboa Park. Later, Mimi told me she thought Aunt Dot seemed a bit peculiar and hoped it didn't run in the family.

The next year Mimi gave birth to Carlton. Mom's weekly letter informed Dot of our new addition Dot in her eccentric way had definite advice for mom on how to help us through what she considered difficult times. She wrote another one of her long letters to my mother that would save our family years of suffering. She had done her research because all the things she wrote about were the current thinking on the care and raising of Mongoloid Children.

Dear Al;

There's something I feel I just must tell you. I'm not member of your family---- haven't considered that for years and nobody else ever did, so I say this only as an outsider whose experience may be useful. I leave it to your judgment whether to pass it on or not, but if, in passing through life we accumulate any experience which might spare suffering to the young and inexperienced it would be cruel to withhold it. Years ago a middle-aged couple who used to live in one of these canyon houses had a little Mongoloid baby. They had a very bright girl of 12.and a boy of 10 when this little one was born. When the doctor told them about the baby and suggested that they put it in Fairview at Costa Mesa where such babies (in San Diego County) are cared for they were at first devastated and then indignant. They just couldn't part with the little helpless thing which they felt needed them so much more than a normal infant. The doctor explained that the people who undertake to work in institutions like the above do so because they love the work, are fitted for it temperamentally and emotionally, are trained for the purpose, are dedicated to it, and are far more understanding and competent than any amateurs, however loving, could be. This made no impression on the X family, who not realizing what they were up against, felt that they could not part from the baby or let anyone else take over its care. But as time went by they began to understand. The mother of such a child, if she undertakes to look after it at home, is trapped for life. She can't leave it for one moment, nor can she get a baby-sitter who will stay with that kind of a baby. It takes a specially trained person. The mother will never have one moments rest, or relief, or relaxation. When the child is a middle-aged man she will still be waiting on him, and the grave problems posed by his maturity will still be on the parents' shoulders. They will have no life of their own at all, unless they can afford a nurse, and the expense of raising such a child is so much greater than that for normal children that almost no one could afford such help. Any illness of the mother is a major catastrophe in a household of this kind. Even in the X household where there was a big girl to help it caused insoluble problems. Then there is the effect on the normal children. To say that it will give them a wonderful opportunity of cultivating understanding and self-sacrifice is to expect of children far, far more than they are capable of sustaining. A situation that requires every ounce of wisdom and fortitude the parents can muster is just too much for children. In addition, there are serious disadvantages to the normal children from several directions. First, there is the cruelty of other children, which cannot be controlled. Second, there is the psychological atmosphere which throws a shadow across the precious days of childhood. Third, there is the fact that the mother has no choice but to scrimp on the attention due her other children in order to have time for the little unfortunate. Fourth, there is the heavy expense which can only be met by deprivation elsewhere in the family. In the past all this was something which had to be borne, because there was no alternative. But that isn't so today. None of the above is any longer necessary. Scientific study of these children and their needs has found the answers. It isn't as if, in surrendering the child, the parents were condemning it to a worse existence. If that were true many parents would prefer to make the life-long sacrifice of caring for the child themselves. As a matter of fact, his existence will be much happier than at home. The

> sense of loss, which would make a normal child miserable, is unknown to him. His affections quickly adjust themselves to whoever is kind to him, but he isn't able to distinguish between that and parental love. As he grows older and needs expert care there are dedicated souls who go into this work simply because they love it, as Ann Sullivan went into the work of training Helen Keller. <u>They choose the work.</u> They know how to bring to the patient whatever healthy satisfaction he is capable of experiencing. He will be able to get the maximum to which he can respond out of life, which would be impossible in the hands of harried and untrained parents. The sooner the baby is relinquished the better. The longer Mimi and Carl keep him the harder the decision will be. My advice is that they get in touch immediately (if the boy is actually found to be deficient) with Pacific State Hospital at Pomona. Carl will be expected to pay something for the baby's keep if he is able. They make every allowance, though, and in Carl's situation wouldn't expect much. In any case, it would be far less than if the baby were raised at home. I'm sure that intelligent young people like Carl and Mimi will see the wisdom of meeting the situation in this way. They need the word from an older person and that's where your love for them may be able to spare them much tribulation. They are young and inexperienced. For us to withhold any knowledge we have on the grounds of not interfering would be stupid and cowardly. The final decision devolves upon them, but any help we can give them is our responsibility to give.

We took Dot's advice with a grain of salt. We thought of all the other advice we had received from her throughout the years and decided to do the best we could and keep her aware of what was happening with Carlton without telling her too much. I kept thinking back to my briefcase and the Café Del Rey Moro and knew she meant well but her judgment left a lot to be desired.

When Carlton was a year old, Dot decided to visit her family in Crestline. This caused quite a stir. None of us had a clue on how to entertain my Dad's sister. Dad said we could put her up in a garage some place, preferably in far off Riverside. My mom in her quiet way said "Now Paul" and that took care of it. We found her a place to stay and made her visit most pleasant. She had a wonderful time and was able to meet her little helpless defective grand nephew Carlton. She fell in love with him and they became bosom buddies. When she returned to San Diego she wrote another letter to mom. This one much more upbeat and with a completely different outlook on the meaning of Carlton's existence;

Dear Al;

Since coming down from Crestline I've been thinking of little Carlton. I suppose most people would say that for a beautiful little boy like that to be born defective is a tragedy. But the more I think of how the pattern of life works out the clearer it seems that nothing is purposeless. It may be that he is very fortunate in this incarnation to be withdrawn from the hullabaloo and pressure of today's living, Maybe his spirit needs this period of retreat in order to emerge stronger and better conditioned for the problems of the next incarnation. For of course, to him his life is as full and interesting, within its limits, as ours is to us. And it is completely free of tensions, worries, disillusionments, and fears that goad so many humans these days. Perhaps his last life was full of responsibility and heavy problems, and Nature has decided that, in addition to his period of fulfillment and replenishment on the other side, he needs a further brief space-----(for any single life-time is a very brief space indeed) of tranquility over here before getting back into harness. You see, the way his life looks to him is entirely different from the way it looks to us on the outside. We see the mental inadequacy and it looks to us like a terrible deprivation. But, after all, the mental or "brain mind" is only an inefficient instrument through which the real mind functions while we're on the physical plane. If the instrument is impaired it has no effect at all upon our real mind which is so much greater than the brain-mind that you might describe the latter as a small pinnacle of ice rising out of a vast submerged ice-berg. During this incarnation Carlton's real mind is held in abeyance somewhat as ours is when we gaze out of a window in a brown study, actually seeing and thinking nothing, just relaxing. When he passes over his full mind will return, as with all of us, and in his next coming all the intellectual qualities he has built up in previous lives will draw him into an appropriate environment. Now to him this life is a happy and desirable one as long as he is surrounded by love. The only thing that could frustrate or hurt him would be the withdrawal of love. As long as he has that he has everything. No fears or disappointments can penetrate except as passing flashes as long as he knows that somebody loves him. That is security. He is blessedly free from the pitfalls and ordeals of life. This must be necessary for him at this time. After this time will go forward all the faster for the respite. So actually from little Carlton's point of view this is a good life. No one should feel sorry for him. We might also say he is fortunate.

Dot never made it back to Crestline but we were able to visit her in San Diego. We had some pleasant visits with her in her little cottage in Normal Heights overlooking the mission. The electric car was still plugged in and she still had her many causes especially the handicapped. She had become a reader for the blind and a friend to anyone in need. She had a special place in her heart for Carlton. Dot always asked about him and felt a special bonding between them.

In 1961 Dot became frail. She still read everything and kept abreast of what was going on in the world. Her causes were still her life. As her condition worsened, we tried to get down to San Diego to comfort her and let her know that her family was there for her. She had made all her own funeral arrangements leaving little notes and directions to follow in case of the demise of Dorothy L Smith.

Mimi, Carlton, my mom and I went down to see Dot for one last time. Carlton seemed to be her soul mate. He'd smile and gurgle and somehow communicate with her. She in turn would talk lovingly with him. After a short visit, we took Carlton out to the backyard. We asked Mom to watch him while Mimi and I took a walk. It was a beautiful San Diego afternoon as we walked around the canyon overlooking the San Diego Mission. When we returned to the house, there was Mom still enjoying the view. We asked her where Carlton was and she said, "Right here with me". We all looked at "right here" but could see no sign of the boy. Panic set in, Carlton could not answer our calls. He had always insisted on being found. We looked high and low for him. We looked in the canyon, out in the front and out in the side by the garage. Finally we looked into Dot's house. There he was on her bed having a grand old time with his grand old aunt. Carlton was smiling and laughing and so was she. That night Dot died in her sleep. She left this world on a high note, having crowned a new young prince, Carlton.

OH DOCTOR

Carlton in the bath, one of his favorite places to be -12 years old

Carlton came into contact with many doctors over the years. Dealing with doctors has been an enlightening experience for us. Some we've grown to love and respect, others have given us cause to wonder.

Carlton was born with a runny nose. This was been a concern of every doctor he came to know. No need to describe a runny nose, but the color of the run was the clue to Carlton's health. What ran out of Carlton's nose immediately told Mimi and me the type of medical emergency we had on our hands. This intuition has caused many doctors to recognize that Mimi and I are a force to be reckoned with, either as extremely perceptive or overly protective parents.

When Carlton was an infant, many in the medical profession knew nothing about children with Down's syndrome. When Carlton was sick, we had to do some detective work to find out what was wrong. Since he did not talk, the doctor had to search for a cause. These searches for what ailed Carlton separated doctors who cared - from doctors who merely practiced medicine.

Carlton's first doctor was Dr. Atkinson, the general practitioner that delivered him. Carlton was the first Mongoloid Dr. Atkinson had ever seen and the last baby he delivered. Before Carlton was released from the hospital, Dr. Atkinson referred us to Dr. Wilson, an infant development specialist, for a diagnostic evaluation. In a cold and abrupt businesslike manner, Dr. Wilson diagnosed Carlton as a Mongoloid and told us to institutionalize him. Mimi and I weren't ready for that. We took Carlton back home to Crestline and to Dr. Atkinson.

Carlton and Dr. Atkinson got along very well. When Carlton went to see Dr. Atkinson, he would let the doctor check him out without any hesitation. If his throat needed looking at he'd let Dr. Atkinson look at it. Dr. Atkinson was Carlton's friend and Carlton was Dr. Atkinson's model patient. For his first seven years Dr. Atkinson kept Carlton healthy, extracting toys and other edibles from his throat, medicating the family for his pinworms and prescribing antibiotics and aspirin as needed. When Doc Atkinson retired he recommended Dr. Allen Sterling for our family.

Dr. Sterling delivered our other three children and nurtured them through the early years of their lives. He had a magical way with Carlton. His concern for our family became more pronounced when Mimi was diagnosed as a type I diabetic. Her health then became his primary concern. He knew Carlton had a major effect on her health. He forewarned us that in time we might have to find a placement for Carlton, adding, "You'll know when that time comes."

When we left Crestline for San Diego we left our friend Dr. Sterling. By then Carlton had left home and was placed in Pacific State Hospital. At that time California was in the process of deinstutionalizing its retarded population and so Carlton was placed in the home of Gladys Belleheumer. When Gladys, because of no physical support from the state, had to give up her six severely handicapped boys, Carlton was moved to Hilldale, a large residential care facility in San Diego. For all that time we had no contact with his doctors.

A doctor came to Hilldale to examine the residents once a month. The doctor saw the residents on an assembly line basis. He looked them over briefly and then spent a great deal of time filling out paperwork. We had no contact with him. We did call the doctor once about a particular problem Carlton was having. We explained the problem as we saw it. His reply was "Carlton who?" Another parent at Hilldale went in to find out how her daughter's health was. The doctor told her that her son was doing fine. The family took their daughter to their own doctor from that point on.

We weren't aware that we could include Carlton on our Kaiser Health Plan until one night when a nurse from Hilldale called to tell us Carlton was sick. He had a high fever and made sounds as if he were ill. The Hilldale doctor was unavailable. The nurse urged us to take him to our own doctor.

We took Carlton to the emergency room at Kaiser. When Dr. Alan Harris, the doctor on duty, examined Carlton's ear, he discovered it was inflamed. He prescribed some medicine and told us he would like to see Carlton in his office in two weeks. Dr. Harris remained Carlton's doctor for the next fifteen years until he decided that Carlton was a little too old for a pediatrician.

Since monthly checkups are mandated by the State, Dr. Harris scheduled a thirty minute appointment for Carlton each month. When Carlton felt good, the examination went smoothly. When Carlton felt bad, he wouldn't let anyone near him. Over the years Dr. Harris, his nurses and I became experts on examining a severely handicapped person, namely Carlton. Sometimes it was a one man job. Dr. Harris checked ears, nose, throat and whole body with complete cooperation from the examinee.

At the worst times it would take Dr. Harris, myself and two or three nurses to hold Carlton down so the doctor could do what had to be done. Whenever we needed an army to hold Carlton, Dr. Harris would warn everyone to protect themselves because if Carlton got hold of any part of their body he would never let go. If Carlton didn't want to open his mouth or let Dr. Harris take blood or check his ears, we had to rally the troops. I held Carlton's head while the nurses held Carlton's arms and legs. Carlton was strong. Sometimes we'd have to have a nurse on each leg. When Carlton was frightened or anxious he could lift a person off the floor by raising his leg.

When we had a multiple person examination, it took place on the floor of the doctor's office. Once everybody was at their examination battle stations, Dr. Harris, stethoscope in hand, began the examination. When finished, we all let go of Carlton. I held him on my lap while he calmed down. While sitting there, he grabbed everything within his reach, on several occasions, Carlton managed to grab the stethoscope around Dr. Harris's neck and Dr. Harris found himself kneeling on the floor struggling for breath. In time we became accustomed to Carlton's moves and could anticipate them.

When Dr. Harris saw Carlton and me in the waiting room, he peeked in through the door and asked, "Is Carlton ready to see me yet?" Because of Carlton's strength and the absence of any body fat Dr. Harris frequently referred to him as the Incredible Hulk. Dr. Harris felt that pound for pound, Carlton was as strong a person as he had ever seen. A rabid Charger fan, He would tell everyone if the Chargers had people like Carlton, they'd be winners.

In the years with Dr. Harris we were able to get urine samples, stool samples and blood samples using our advanced techniques. Sometimes the samples we got weren't exactly what we were looking for, but Carlton gave them to us anyway.

Dr. Harris and I were constantly amazed at the way this silent patient could keep us all in such a state of anxiety. Sometimes our greatest examination plan blew up in our face because Carlton decided to have a bowel movement or to urinate. No matter what Carlton did, Dr. Harris and I would always have an alternate strategy. Carlton lived to be forty so our plans must have worked.

Throughout the years Carlton's nose continued to run. The nurses and aides at Hilldale were concerned. Dr. Harris was concerned. Finally, when Carlton was fifteen and a muscular ninety pounds, Dr. Harris recommended Carlton see an eye, nose and throat specialist. Knowing Carlton, Dr. Harris chose the head of the Eye, Nose and Throat department to see if he could stem the flow. Dr. Harris told the doctor of Carlton's special needs and that he wasn't always cooperative. He assured him that one of Carlton's parents would be there to help. He even explained our methods of examining Carlton.

Mimi took Carlton for his eye, nose and throat examination. In the examining room, the nurse told Mimi to put Carlton in the chair, the doctor would join them momentarily. Leaving Carlton on a chair in a doctor's office is like turning the proverbial bull loose in a china shop. There were so many gadgets and hoses hanging around that after just one minute of Carlton's time, it would have taken months to straighten out the carnage. Mimi held him on her lap.

The doctor came into the room with his stethoscope around his neck and his eye examining lens on his glasses. He greeted Carlton in a fatherly way and seemed surprised to get no response. He asked Mimi to place Carlton in the examination chair. Mimi tried to tell him that that wouldn't work but the doctor wasn't listening. So she put Carlton in the chair. The doctor started to take Carlton's pulse. Before he was able to get his hand around Carlton's wrist, Carlton had the stethoscope. Wrenching Carlton's hands off the scope, Mimi managed to free the doctor. She suggested that she hold Carlton's hands while the doctor examined him. The specialist conceded that this might work. Mimi stood behind the chair holding Carlton's hands behind him as the doctor pulled up a swivel stool in front of Carlton. He sat on the stool in his best doctor position, stethoscope poised, tongue depressor at the ready and legs spread for balance. Carlton was struggling a bit as the doctor began aggressively moving in. Mimi tried to tell him to back off a minute until they had the situation under control. The doctor kept moving in. Mimi had a good grip on Carlton's arms but no one had his feet. Carlton gave a kick and the doctor flew two feet in the air. The force of Carlton's kick sent the doctor spinning around on his swivel stool. He was in mortal pain. Red faced and barely breathing through his clenched teeth, the doctor mumbled that the examination was finished.

The next time we took Carlton to see Dr. Harris, he laughed. The ear, nose and throat specialist had told Dr. Harris to say he didn't feel comfortable having Carlton as a patient. Dr. Harris assured him that he understood. He told us, as an aside, that the specialist was now singing soprano in his church choir.

Later, the same specialist did operate on Carlton's nose and place tubes in his ears. He even grew to like Carlton especially when he was anesthetized.

Carlton's nose still ran but the running slowed to a walk. He still had periodic episodes with his ears. These maladies were just part of his life.

We've had our share of doctors representing Casablanca Corporation which owned Hilldale. Some were dedicated to the good health of the residents; others were more interested in making the corporation look good. It was one of the latter that almost did in the parent group that we had formed his name was Dr. Pullman, he was the medical director of the Casablanca Corporation.

Our parent group had been in existence for six years at the time, with our number one concern the health of our children. Cleanliness was lax. Portable toilets were left in the rooms, uncleaned. Shigilla (a type of contagious diarrhea) raged through the facility periodically. Sometimes an outbreak would last for weeks, during which time we couldn't visit our children. Everyone living at Hilldale seemed to be sick most of the time. Rumors that some residents were carriers of Hepatitis turned out to be true. We learned that anyone who had lived in a state hospital was a carrier of Hepatitis. We were given no information concerning the health care of our children. We had many questions that were not answered.

The parents began to complain, first to Hilldale's administrator Mrs. Mumford then to Licensing. Licensing came in, found many regulations being disregarded and wrote up citations accordingly. Hilldale was fined for health code violations. The relationship between Hilldale and the parents hit an all-time low. I explained to Mrs. Mumford that all we wanted was information and openness. We had turned to Licensing as a last resort. We needed a response to our concerns. She angrily told me that Hilldale always considered the parents first when any decision was made and was sorry that I didn't see that.

I asked her if Dr. Pullman, the medical director, would come to our next meeting to answer some of our questions. Mrs. Mumford made arrangements for him to come to our next monthly meeting. I contacted all the parents in the San Diego area. The response was overwhelming; parents of two thirds of the residents were present at that meeting. They voiced their concerns and anger before the doctor or anyone from Hilldale arrived. They were unhappy and they wanted change. Thirty minutes after the meeting started, Mrs. Mumford, the head nurse and Dr. Pullman marched in. I welcomed them and explained what we hoped to accomplish. Before I could go into any detail, Dr. Pullman took the microphone and ranted, "If you people don't get off our backs, we'll close Hilldale and send your sons and daughters all over the state of California!" He closed his tirade by asking God to have mercy on our souls. He turned and, with Mrs. Mumford and the head nurse, marched out of the room.

Many of the parents panicked. Some, afraid that their child would be sent away, said they would never complain again. Because of Dr. Pullman's threats, some of the parents stopped being involved with the parent group. They were terrified that Hilldale might close. The next day I told Mrs. Mumford that our sons and daughters would probably be better off if Casablanca Corporation did close Hilldale.

However, in spite of the medical director's threats, we were accorded better access. Slowly the medical situation improved but no parent who had a son or daughter there thought it would ever be perfect.

Sometimes hospitalization was necessary. Hospital care often was well intentioned but inadequate due to a lack of training for hospital staff in dealing with persons with severe Developmental Disablities.

Carlton was born at Santa Anita Hospital at Lake Arrowhead. He was treated as a premature infant and placed in an oxygen enriched environment for the first two weeks of his life. We were always fond of that little hospital because of the friendliness and loving concern of its staff.

While Carlton was living at home in Crestline, the only available hospital was Saint Bernardines in San Bernardino. Dr. Sterling placed Carlton there for his bout with diarrhea. He was there for the five days. While he was there he was so weak that he was easily managed. When he came home, he still had diarrhea and he was still weak. Although the nurses at St. Bernardines were caring, we felt the hospital could have done much more medically. He apparently was sent home before he was ready because he was retarded.

When Carlton needed emergency treatment, we took him to St. Bernadine's. I dreaded going to the emergency room. Carlton wasn't brought in on a stretcher so they ignored him for more obvious emergencies and got to him when they could. Often Carlton and I waited for hours for a medical procedure that only took a couple of minutes.

We never considered Pacific State Hospital a hospital. From the day we first saw it until the day Carlton left, we viewed it as a holding tank for retarded children. Even if a child got sick, he remained in the ward, infecting the other children as he tried to get well. Mimi and I saw nothing at Pacific State that even suggested it was a hospital.

When Carlton moved to San Diego he spent time in four different hospitals, Kaiser, Children's, Grossmont and Paradise Hills. Most of the treatment he received was outpatient. When he had tubes placed in his ears or a minor operation, he was in and out in one day. When he needed outpatient care Mimi and I accompanied him. The nurses at Kaiser depended on us to help them with the pre-op routine. We stayed with Carlton while they took his temperature, blood pressure and whatever tests were necessary. We kept him calm while the anesthesiologist prepared him for surgery. We waited for him in the recovery room so he would see familiar faces when he came out of the anesthetic. When he was alert, the ambulance would take him back to Hilldale.

In time the nurses came to know Carlton and were always happy to see him. They also made Mimi and me feel we were an important part of the healing process. For Carlton and for us, Kaiser Hospital was by far the most hospitable hospital.

Unfortunately, dentistry was not performed at Kaiser. Once a dentist diagnosed Carlton's dental needs, he submitted them to the state for funding. Once funding was approved, the dentist reserved operating space at one of the local hospitals. Mimi and I always went with Carlton to these appointments but we were never made welcome. We were treated as outsiders, asked to wait outside. We insisted on staying with Carlton during the prep. We knew he needed to see familiar faces.

The Children's Hospital was the first hospital he went to for dental care. He was to spend the night there. Mimi and I took him to the hospital, filled out the papers and went with him to his room. Another child in the room was breathing oxygen and being fed interveiniously. A nurse placed Carlton in his bed and said she'd be right back. We explained to her that Carlton didn't understand what she was saying. We also told her that he would get out of his bed and playfully destroy anything he could get his hands on. The nurse paid no attention so Mimi and I stayed with him.

Knowing Carlton's needs, Mimi took him to the bathroom adjoining his room. She noticed a large container of urine on the back of the toilet and put it in a safe place. Later she told the nurse about the urine and asked why it was left there. We explained again that Carlton could get out of bed and get into things like that. The nurse didn't answer, but she did take the bottle and its contents away.

We knew we couldn't stay with Carlton all night so we went to the nurse's station with our concerns. We were told not to worry. We said we wouldn't worry if someone would at least come with us and review the situation. A nurse agreed. When we entered the room, we found Carlton was out of his bed and playing with the oxygen tanks that belonged to the child in the next bed. The nurse gasped as I picked up Carlton and placed him back in his bed. We pointed out all the assorted equipment that was sure to entice Carlton. The nurse recognized the gravity of the situation, but said it was against hospital policy to restrain a child. However, she decided to make an exception in Carlton's case and immediately placed netting over his bed. Carlton had his dental work done the next day without any further incident.

Each time Carlton was hospitalized for dentistry, we encountered similar situations. Each time we were asked to wait outside while the nurses took care of the pre-op routine. Our suggestions went unheard. When things got out of hand, we were invited to help. Once the situation calmed and Carlton was anesthetized, we were asked to wait outside until the procedure was completed. When the dental work was done they promised to come to get us. Sometimes they forgot. Once Mimi waited to see the dentist until after six o'clock only to find out that the dentist had left and Carlton had returned to Hilldale three hours earlier.

Our experience with the medical profession and hospitals is not unique. Severely Developmentally Disabled persons are a small percentage of patients seen by doctors or placed in hospital care. There is little training for medical personnel concerning this population. Mimi and I have learned all we know from experience. Fortunately for many doctors and nurses, we shared that experience with them when they were willing to listen.

FOOD FOR THOUGHT

Carlton (22 years old) and I (at 50). Carlton is ready to dig in!

Food, food, wonderful food has always been a part of Carlton's life. Maybe not food itself as much as eating food. While you and I are thinking about the food in front of us, Carlton eats it. He enjoys anything that's edible as long as it isn't smoked oysters.

Mimi and I suffered through Carlton's first feedings, sterilizing bottles, filling them with formula, watching him slowly drain their life-giving contents. He was a slow eater, so slow in fact that feeding seemed to be one continuous action, once one bottle was empty it was time for another.

We never knew whether Carlton was getting enough milk. He never cried, so we just kept feeding him. In time, as we gained confidence, feeding became a matter of routine. I enlarged the hole in the nipple to speed the process along. Carlton grew and so did his appetite. It wasn't long before Mimi and I realized we had an eating machine on our hands. Once Carlton discovered foods other than milk nothing was safe. He tried eating everything, food, toys, dirt, trees, paper and grass, anything he could sink his teeth into.

Carlton was never a neat eater so most of his meals were what we called "shared". He shared them with the world around him. When Colleen and Tommy came along in 1961, "shared" became a way of life for our family. A bottle lost was a bottle found. Some child was sure to pick it up and finish off its contents. Mimi and I only hoped that the bottle was lost on the same day it was found.

Carlton at two eating

When baby foods and baby cereals dominated the menu for the Smith children, "shared" took on a whole new meaning. Carlton, Colleen and Tom shared their food with each other, the floor, the ceiling, the walls, their stuffed animals and any other household item alive or manufactured. We had a real mess on our hands.

Mimi and I saw the handwriting on the wall. Actually it was the food on the wall that mandated change. We had a wonderful back deck, built high off the ground, surrounded by trees. It was there that we entertained company and let the kids play. We decided to use it as an outdoor dining room. We had privacy and the children shared their meals with the birds and the other animals. After each meal we got out the hose and washed down the area, kids and all.

Carlton at 3 enjoying a meal on the outside deck

In time Colleen and Tom learned to get food from their plates to their mouths and we were able to eat our meals inside again. Carlton never really mastered the art of neat eating, but we maneuvered him through each formal eating time with tight parental supervision. This worked fine. It was the rest of the time, the time between breakfast, lunch and dinner that proved to be our downfall.

Sometimes it's hard to imagine how someone like Carlton can survive in this world. He never cried when he was hungry. He never asked for food. He lived in a silent world. Mimi and I watched over him and made sure his needs were met, but we weren't always on top of things. He kept us in a constant state of confusion. When Carlton was our only child, he didn't have to fend for himself. We were always there. When the other children came on the scene, his survival instincts were honed. He had to hold his own with his sister and brother. He did this in subtle ways. He developed a knack for being in the right place at the right time. He also kept things hopping by using the fastest hands in the world to grab anything within reach.

One day Mimi was out with her friends and I was in charge of the noon day meal. Tommy was in his nip and nap and Colleen and Carlton in their high chairs. I filled their bottles, fixed their baby foods and began filling my children with food and milk. They were like baby birds, mouths open and ready for food. I kept shoveling it in, missing every now and then, but always close. The whole process took about fifteen to twenty minutes. When the meal was completed, I was exhausted but proud of a job well done.

I started cleaning up the debris, enjoying the happiness of fatherhood and the exhilaration of another meal accomplished. There was Colleen looking contented, ready to get down and begin a new adventure. There was Carlton smiling, looking satisfied as only Carlton can look after eating a scrumptious meal. And finally there was Tommy looking like a starving birdling, clean as a whistle and eagerly awaiting his food.

I realized I had missed him. No wonder Carlton looked so satisfied. I had fed him twice. I fed Tom and wonder how many times Tommy missed his food due to brotherly appetite and parental oversight.

It is those fast hands and being in the right place at the right time that helped Carlton get more than his share of food through the years. People who knew him kept a constant vigil over their food or drink. They knew it would be in his mouth so quickly that they'd never see it vanish. I've seen food disappear from a fork while it was on the way to a mouth. Carlton was blessed with great food snatching techniques.

On holidays Mimi always put out snacks for our guests. On one of these special occasions she put out a platter of smoked oysters. The children played, the adults visited, and Carlton spotted an opportunity. He saw those oysters unattended. He attacked. He grabbed one, ate it, and didn't like it. The next thing we knew there were smoked oysters all over the ceiling, floor and family. From that little episode we learned that Carlton did not like smoked oysters, and that he was going to make sure that nobody else would have to eat them. We smelled and found smoked oysters hither and yon for weeks after that holiday. We haven't served them since.

Then there was the half gallon of maraschino cherries. Mimi had been tutoring a child who was homebound. To show her appreciation the child's mother gave Mimi a huge jar of cherries. We had no use for them. We didn't like maraschino cherries. One day, for some unknown reason, Mimi left the open jar on the countertop within Carlton's reach. He reached, ate one cherry and dumped the rest on the floor. He then decided to be an artist and used the corner of our kitchen as his personal canvas. Using a variety of techniques, he smeared maraschino cherry juice on walls, furniture, floor and self. The whole process took less than a minute. We stuck to everything we touched for weeks. When we got the cherries, we wondered what we were going to do with them. Carlton solved our problem in a way we never would have thought of ourselves. If he hadn't taken the initiative, we'd still be trying to think of what to do with them.

When Carlton turned four, Mimi made him a special birthday cake adorned with red and blue frosting with animals, a merry-go-round and four birthday candles. It was a masterpiece. Mimi asked me to watch the cake while she fixed the table for the birthday celebration. I watched the cake but I forgot to watch Carlton. He moved in like a vulture and got two handfuls of Mimi's masterpiece right in front of my eyes. I yelled, "No No Carlton"! But it was too late. The damage had been done. The cake was a disaster. Mimi tried to camouflage the huge crater in the cake but it was useless. We went on with the celebration as if nothing had happened. We sat at table, the four of us and Carlton, his face full of red and blue frosting and proceeded to celebrate four years of chaos.

By four, Carlton was in the habit of putting anything in his mouth that appealed to him. When he was playing outdoors he ate dirt, flowers, leaves or anything else that looked edible. When we saw the telltale signs of his snacking, we washed him up and hoped for the best. Instead of the best, he frequently came up with a case of pinworms. When Carlton had pinworms the whole family had to be treated. The treatment for pinworms was a horrible tasting liquid. It was administered to every member of the family according to the person's weight. I being the largest member of the family ended up taking the largest dose, usually about ten or twelve tablespoons of the stuff. I became paranoid every time Carlton went outside, dreading another series of ten or twelve tablespoons of that horrible medicine. Paranoia or not, twice a year, like clockwork, we got dewormed.

One evening we went to a local restaurant with friends and took all the kids as a special treat. I held Carlton on my lap to avoid any problems. The waitress took our order and served the salads. When she placed a turntable with four bowls of salad dressing on the table I could see trouble ahead. Carlton liked spinning things. Before I could warn the waitress not to put it down, old "fast hands" had the spinning tray up in the air and on top of his head. Thousand Island, French, Italian and Sour Cream dressings were dripping all over. Salad dressing covered the seat and worked its way down between the cushions. Carlton and I crept out, went home and enjoyed a meal of leftovers. Mimi and the rest of the party finished their meal in what she described as a very somber atmosphere. We didn't attempt any more family excursions to restaurants regardless of what other families were doing.

Eating wasn't limited to a homebound activity with Carlton; he ate wherever the good Lord placed food. Mimi developed a great shopping technique. When she went shopping, she put Carlton in the shopping cart and kept the cart in the middle of the aisle and her purchases under Carlton's feet so he couldn't reach either the shelves or the food in the cart. Every once in a while she got too close to the shelves and ended up with various surprise purchases at the checkout stand.

One day as she rounded the corner of the aisle, she met a man coming around from the other side. As the shopping carts came together, Carlton reached in the gentleman's basket, grabbed a package of ham, took a bite, cellophane and all, and threw it back. The man was dumbfounded. He looked at Mimi, he looked at Carlton, and he looked at his ham and just shook his head. Mimi smiled and told him that Carlton sometimes did that. Carlton sat in his cart innocently chewing his ham. On another occasion a woman saw Carlton in his shopping cart and felt sorry for him. She gave him a dollar. He ate it instantly. I thanked the lady and told her we'd watch out for it. We never found it but the thought crossed our minds that there might be a way to market our son. We could put him in a shopping cart and go from market to market looking confused and stressed out. We figured we'd never have to buy food for Carlton and we could accumulate some cash. We often wonder what our life style would be today if we had only followed through with the idea.

Easter was a special time at our house. We dyed Easter eggs and decorated the house. After the kids were asleep, Mimi and I filled Easter baskets with chocolate bunnies, chocolate eggs, marshmallow chicks and jelly beans. We'd hide them in the living room. In the morning the search was on. When someone found a basket, squeals of delight echoed through the house. Each year Carlton's basket was hidden in the same place, on top of the living room table. He always checked that table for food so it was a natural finding place. At the conclusion of the Easter basket hunt, we gave instructions on how to eat the Easter goodies conservatively. We told the kids that if they ate only one chocolate a day, their baskets would last for more than three weeks and memories of this joyous day would last forever. After our moving words, the kids proceeded to eat everything as fast as they could without getting caught. We made Carlton's basket a little less ample. He couldn't count so we felt we could short him without any repercussions. We gave him hard boiled eggs because they were better for him. At least that was our theory until we heard the first crunch; he was eating his eggs shell and all.

Carlton's eating habits often led us to seek medical help. Once he was playing out on the porch when he started to choke. We couldn't see the problem so we took him to Dr. Atkinson's office. The doctor probed cautiously and then pulled out the steering wheel of a toy jeep. Carlton had been playing with his toys and unfortunately had decided to give the wheel the taste test. When Dr. Atkinson pulled out the steering wheel, he looked at us with a twinkle in his eye and asked Carlton where the rest of the jeep was. When we got home, the first thing we checked was the back porch to see if the rest of the jeep was still there. It was.

One day when he was playing in the yard, he began choking so I rushed him down the hill to the hospital emergency room. I gave them all the particulars about Carlton and what I knew about his choking. They told me to wait. "Please hurry! My son is choking" I begged them. Time went by. No one came to help. I told them I was getting scared. The nurse directed me to another room and said the doctor would be with us shortly.

Again we waited. While we were waiting, Carlton had occasional periods of choking and coughing and was turning pale. I knew he needed help. I went out and demanded Carlton be seen. The nurse appeared to be surprised that we were still there. I heard a doctor being paged over the hospital speaker system. The doctor appeared, made some flimsy excuse and proceeded to extract a piece of cedar from Carlton's throat. Carlton's color returned immediately. He had been eating a branch from a tree and a small portion had lodged in his throat. We had been in the emergency room for over four hours for a procedure that took less than two minutes.

On the way home I thought about the hopelessness of being a parent of a child like Carlton. The people at the hospital didn't hear me when I told them my son was choking. It didn't bother them that I was scared. If the child wasn't crying, he must be all right. The parent is just over precautious.

When I received a bill for four hours of emergency room time and an hour of doctor's time, I was furious. I went down and explained to them what I would do if they even thought about having me pay for that outrage. They started to protest but cooler heads prevailed. They apologized and tore up the bill.

Carlton lived to be forty. With all the wrong things he had eaten, he still must have eaten something right. He was strong, he was healthy and he still grabbed food off of other peoples' plates until the day he died.

He never had a second chance at smoked oysters or maraschino cherries. He learned to eat his own food with a fork and a spoon. At Hilldale where he lived, they knew from experience to keep food of any kind a safe distance from him, for in Carlton's case, wherever there is food there is no time for thought.

ARE WE THERE YET?

The Birthday card Dad made for Mimi and we were headed out on our grand adventure

"Did you bring the bottles?" "Have we got all the kids?" We were young and we were about to begin one of those youthful adventures that to us seemed so wise and rational. At the time to our elders it seemed ridiculous and stupid. This magical adventure, ridiculous and stupid though it might have appeared, took place in the summer of 1963 when Carlton was four, Colleen was two and a half and Tommy was one and a half. Mimi and I decided it was time to visit her mom and dad in upstate New York. It would be a great opportunity to see the country and grow together as a family. We could drive across the United States, stopping here and there, seeing the great wonders of our country: the Grand Canyon, the Petrified Forest, Carlsbad Cavern, Mount Rushmore, Yellowstone and any other natural wonder that lay between California and Buffalo New York. What an opportunity for our family! And we could do it cheap because our VW Bug got great gas mileage.

In fact the way I figured it, even with the extra miles we'd travel, we could make it back to Buffalo for less than fifty bucks. The price was right, the plan was perfect. We'd see the country and visit grandpa and grandma.

Preparations began in April. I purchased a luggage rack for our bug so that we could take some clothes and things along with us. The kids were all in different stages of diapers. Carlton was older, but severely developmentally disabled, Tommy was still little more than an infant and Colleen was old enough to be trained but smart enough to want the same treatment and the same amount of attention as her two brothers. For this same reason they were all on bottles. We figured this was an asset as it would save us a lot of clothes sorting and menu making.

I cut out a piece of plywood to cover the back seat area, so we could put some of our supplies on the floor beneath it. The kids would then have a kind of playpen in the back where they could play, sleep and generally enjoy each other's company. Safety seats were unknown at the time. Had they been known this whole silly idea of a VW cross country excursion with three kids in diapers and on bottles would have been nipped in the bud. By June all was in readiness. I showed our travel home to my mom and dad, family and friends and they all shook their heads in what we thought was adulation. We know now that it wasn't adulation at all. It was wonderment. They were wondering to themselves," Are they too dumb to see? Are they blind? If we say something will they be able to hear?" Nothing in life changes. Our kids have grown up and I now find myself thinking, "Are they too dumb to see? Are they blind? If I say something will they be able to hear?" The answers then and now were and still are the same," yes, yes and no."

The day arrived for the great adventure. We had everything packed neatly in numbered suitcases and boxes. We loaded the luggage rack with everything we would need in New York. We covered it in case of rain and hoped to leave it untouched until we triumphantly arrived in grandpa's backyard. We put a lot of stuff on the floor under the children's playpen and hoped we wouldn't need it too often because I didn't want to keep moving the board that covered the back area and disrupting their romper room. We put everything we would need during the trip in the front baggage compartment, food, diapers and basic clothing. We had a small cooler that fit under Mimi's feet in the front seat. All in all we felt that we were traveling first class. My dad made us a special going away card, it was a picture of a VW crammed with luggage and people with a flagpole on top flying three diapers and a sign pointing toward New York.

We put a clean diaper on each kid and gave each one a full bottle. About five that afternoon we headed east so we could make it through the desert at night. Who said we hadn't thought of everything? "Did you turn off the coffee?" Did you bring the disposable diapers?"

We hadn't gone twenty miles before we smelled a definite poo poo smell. I asked Mimi who she thought it might be. She looked back but could not tell by looking so I kept driving as I wanted to get some mileage in before we made our first stop. We'd only been on the road a little more than an hour when the smell got worse. We knew we had a problem. Out of self-preservation we had to stop and change the kids diapers. We thought that with these new fangled disposable diapers we'd be way ahead of the game. No diaper pail, no lingering mess, just take them off and throw them away, the only trouble was the darned things leaked. In all our preparations we didn't plan for leaky diapers. After only an hour on the road we got the feeling that changing leaky diapers might just be a big part of our trip. We stopped near Barstow and made all the necessary changes threw our throw away diapers in the trash cans and were again heading east, radio blaring and dreaming great dreams, oblivious to reality.

We were on our way to Needles where we thought we'd have our first pleasant dining experience. We had packed sandwiches and fruit before we left. We stopped and spread our Indian looking blanket on the grass of a little public park near the highway. It was a good time to stretch. I said to Mimi, "so far so good," and ate my sandwich. The kids ran around a lot. I noticed they didn't eat a whole lot, but I figured with all the excitement of leaving and traveling that was about par for the course. We gave them some fruit, checked their bottles, Carlton blue, Colleen pink, Tommy white, loaded everything back into our bug and were on our way. If the whole trip was going to go as well as our first dinner stop then it was going to be one super great experience. Life just couldn't get much better than that.

We had decided before we left to go as far as we could the first twenty four hours. We drove through the night, only stopping for gas. We thought the kids would sleep most of the night and Mimi would keep me company and awake as we journeyed along. By midnight it was Mimi who fell asleep and the kids who were keeping me awake. There was no way they were going to miss any part of what was going on. I figured it would catch up with them in time, and they'd probably sleep most of the way to New York beginning tomorrow.

As dawn appeared and the first sun shone in the East the odor of dirty diapers filled the car. I knew it was time to make another pit stop. We were now in Arizona where we found a beautiful desert rest area. We again unloaded car and kids, cleaned them up gave them each a bowl of cold cereal and milk, walked around and enjoyed the crisp dry Arizona dawn. We put all the throw away diapers and leftovers in a paper bag, threw it into the trash can, and were again on our way. We opened the windows to air things out. As we were leaving the rest area Colleen, always the sentimentalist, yelled out so everyone in Western Arizona could hear, "Bye bye poo poo." Mimi, considering the size of a VW, did an amazing disappearing act.

Soon we would see our first natural phenomena, the Petrified Forest. On our way we would be able to view the Painted Desert. It would be an experience this family would never forget. Yes, we were on our way again and the world was our oyster. Mimi and I were enjoying a cup of coffee and the kids were enjoying their bottles of milk, Carlton white, Colleen blue and Tommy pink.

We pointed out the Painted Desert and stopped to view this wondrous sight. Mimi and I thought the kids would want to take in all its grandeur and maybe find a particular area of beauty and point it out to mommy and daddy. We in turn would explain and identify its different hues and shades. It never happened. They just wanted to eat cookies and chase each other with handfuls of sand. Mimi and I didn't even get a chance to enjoy the different hues and shades of the Painted Desert. We quickly got back into the bug and headed for the Petrified Forest. We knew the Petrified Forest would get them. As we were driving along I glanced back to see how the kids were doing because they seemed so quiet. They were all contentedly laying back in their cage sucking their bottles, Carlton the pink one, Colleen the white one and Tommy the blue one. "Oh well," I thought, "at least they're quiet.

We made it to the Petrified Forest by lunch time. This was our first real chance to see a natural wonder up close and personal. We got out of the car and went into a small building full of petrified wood and other relics from the past The kids could care less. We went out into the forest area and could see firsthand the petrified wood giants from ages long past. Mimi and I were greatly impressed. The kids took off running except for Carlton who we were carrying along with us. Mimi yelled for Tom and Colleen to come back. They paid no attention to her, they were enjoying themselves too much hiding in this forest of beautifully colored rocks. We finally rounded them up, ate lunch, loaded up our home on wheels and were on our way when Tommy let out a terrible cry. He'd lost his bottle. After a monstrous search we finally found it hidden among the blankets and toys the kids called home. A little shaken but still optimistic we were again on our way, next stop the great crater where a meteorite had hit the earth and created a big hole in the ground.

As we approached the crater we were filled with anticipation. Right in this place a celestial event had taken place eons ago. Here in Arizona, space and earth had come together and we could see the results of that epic event. We got out of the car and entered the site of the crater and there it was, a big hole in the ground. It's hard to put a great deal of meaning to big holes in the ground, especially to little kids. They took one look and Colleen asked, "Where is it?" Mimi and I both said, "The hole is it!" Colleen, of course muttered, as only a two and a half year old can, "The hole is what?!" Rather than get too deeply involved in the type of conversation that would lead to nowhere, we suggested we have a coke. In the meantime, Tommy was trying to fill the big hole up by throwing rocks into it. Colleen decided to join in the fun while Mimi and I were slowly becoming mortified. We took some literature and left. We headed toward New Mexico. All was again calm. Tommy had the blue bottle while Colleen had the other two.

Mimi and I decided that a meandering trip to all the wonders of the United States was ridiculous. From that moment on we would get to New York as soon as was humanly possible. If we happened to come to a landmark or an historical site, Mimi would try to read what it was as we passed. And thus it was as we headed east toward Albuquerque. Fatigue was setting in as we had been on the road a good eighteen hours. I was looking forward to a comfortable motel and a good night's sleep. We stopped for a picnic dinner in Albuquerque. Mimi went shopping for cold cuts, bread, some macaroni salad, some cookies and some milk. It was nice to sit on the grass in the park. The kids could run off some excess energy and Mimi and I could relax for a spell. We decided we'd push on for a few more hours then find a motel and settle in for the night. Then we would clean up and sleep until we woke even if it happened to be late the following afternoon.

We traveled on for another few hours. We had to stop early that evening as my eyes were beginning to close and the car was moving along on pure instinct. We finally found a little old motel in a place called Santa Rosa. There wasn't much there, a garage, an Indian Trading Post and a small roadside cafe. We took a room with two double beds thinking Mimi and I would have one and the kids would have the other.

Mimi decided she would get the kids ready for bed while I rested. Fortunately this motel was old enough to have the shower in a bathtub. She filled the tub and the three kids hopped in and had a wonderful time splashing each other and flooding the place. Before they got out I was zonked. I lay down to rest for a minute and passed out. Mimi got the kids in their pajamas and ready for bed, she tucked them in to go to sleep and then she too lay down to rest for a moment and fell sound asleep.

I remember something waking me up sometime during the night. I jumped up unaware of where I really was and heard a toilet flushing. I staggered into the bathroom and found Colleen having a great old time flushing the toilet over and over. Carlton was in the bathtub pretending he was taking a bath while Tommy was nowhere to be found. I finally located him in our bed sleeping as only a baby can sleep. I located their bottles and explained to them that they had to go to sleep as tomorrow would be another big day on the road. They all looked at me, wide eyed and wide awake, with their bottles in their mouths. I knew that from the looks in their eyes, Mimi and I were in real trouble. I fell back into bed and remember in the deepest part of my unconsciousness, the sound of children's feet running all over the place and the sound of a toilet flushing. I prayed that none of the kids would be in the toilet that night or I'm certain we would have lost one of them before morning. The night passed quickly. I woke up at dawn, refurbished and ready to get on with the great adventure. I showered and dressed and nobody else moved. It was now my turn for sweet revenge. I woke everybody up and announced that breakfast was served. The bowls and plastic spoons were in the car so I gave them all a napkin full of cornflakes a piece of bread and a fresh bottle. Naturally, rather than eat the dry cereal, they went to war with it. They threw it, kicked it, crunched it and did everything you can do with dry cereal but eat it. We knew that our best bet was to load up the bug and get back on the road, even the cramped quarters of our mobile prison was better than what remained of our tidy little motel room. We did just that. We loaded up car and kids, promised we'd stop for a treat in a little while, left a decent tip for the cleaning lady and took off. All was well; we'd made it through the second night. We were on the road again. The kids were calmly sucking on any bottle they wanted to suck on. New York here we come!

Driving along the roads of New Mexico that morning made me forget the motel and look forward to the day ahead. The VW was doing fine. We came to the conclusion that a van or something bigger than a bug would have been nicer. It was much too late to be thinking about such things so we plowed on. The West is pretty flat and pretty bleak. We went by one Indian Trading Post after another. Some were shaped like teepees while others had huge arrows sticking in the ground near them, still others were nestled in among beautifully colored boulders. All advertised souvenirs of the Southwest. All of them seemed to be having sales. We drove on to Tucumcari where we stopped and bought the kids their promised treat. There were a lot of Indian people in Tucumcari. We pointed this out to the kids. Tom and Carlton could have cared less but Colleen's picture of Indians was a far cry from what she was seeing in Tucumcari. She let us know about it too. She kept yelling "where are all the Indians?" We told her that most of the people she saw were Indians. She kept yelling she wanted to see someone with a war bonnet on a horse because that's what Indians were. We told her to eat her candy bar and we'd explain it in the car. We strolled around town looking at the beautiful turquoise jewelry and wonderful crafts. We soon left Tucumcari and New Mexico and entered the great state of Texas.

We knew we were in Texas because there were two pillars beside the road with a sign that said "Welcome to Texas the Lone Star State." These pillars were in the middle of nowhere. I announced this landmark to my fellow travelers, but no one seemed to care. The trip was starting to get boring and uncomfortable. The scenery seemed to be nothing but flat, sandy unending vistas with occasional tumbleweeds skittering across the dusty landscape. The kids started wondering out loud if we were almost there yet. I cheerfully answered "almost, just another seventeen hundred miles or so." We drove by what seemed to be abandoned farms and motels. I would have liked to stop and explore these ghost houses but this was not the time for such adventures. Instead I prayed that the VW would not break down or we might never be heard from again. We finally made it to Amarillo where we stopped for a break. We took a little walk and made all the necessary changes. We ate in a little cafe, our first meal "out". The children enjoyed sitting in a booth for a change. We all ate as much as we wanted then we ordered ice cream for dessert. The kids got some of it in their mouths, the rest they wore out with them. We stopped at a small market and refilled our larder. We filled the kids' bottles which now numbered two (the blue one had disappeared) and headed for Oklahoma.

Carlton on a break during our trip next to the VW. He seems to be expressing what Mimi and I were feeling

There wasn't much difference between Texas and Oklahoma. The land was still flat and dusty. There were a few more small towns so there was a little more to see as we drove along. We decided to drive until dinner time and then call it a day. We got to a town outside Oklahoma City about 6:30 and decided this would be our home for the night. We found a little flea bag of a motel in this place called Clinton. It was a big room with two beds in it. It had a bathroom, but no bathtub. Instead there was a common shower down the hall. It was like a trailer park with no trailers. The area had some of the biggest bugs we ever had the privilege of seeing. The kids were amazed and ready for a scientific expedition to discover the world's biggest bug. Mimi was terrified having been born a hater of anything that crawls on walls or ceilings. Nothing bothered me at that moment, I was too tired. We carefully spread our picnic out on one of the beds (checking to see that what we were not eating bugs). After dinner we took a walk around the place. We found horses out behind the motel fence, lots of other guests around, many of whom seemed permanent and train tracks nearby but no trains in sight. The whole set up seemed a little scary, but it was only for one night, and it did fall within our budget. When we got back to our bungalow we locked the door, got the kids ready for bed and tried to sleep. The trains seem only to run through Oklahoma at night. People seem to walk around all night in Oklahoma. In Oklahoma horses seem to neigh all night. Our motel seemed to be located in the middle of a major highway in Oklahoma. Insects and big bugs buzzed and crawled all night in Oklahoma. I say crawled because we heard them. Needless to say we didn't get the deep restful sleep we had been looking forward to in Oklahoma. We were up at the crack of dawn. We ate a quick breakfast, again checking our food for foreign matter, loaded up and took off, promising never to return this way again.

After our night in Oklahoma it actually felt good to be on the road again. The kids were happily sharing the two remaining bottles. Mimi and I were quietly, almost numbly anticipating another day on the road. For all its bugs, Oklahoma is still a very pretty state to drive through. We drove on the first pay road we had ever encountered. It was strange for me to pay to drive on a "freeway". California was never like this. The drive on the throughway was pleasant and fast. We drove right by Tulsa. My wife pointed Tulsa out to the kids. From there it was on to Missouri. That day we had our first view of the Ozarks. The weather was perfect and the drive through the forests of the Ozarks was awesome. The throughway had come to an end with Oklahoma so a winding highway lead us to Joplin where we stopped briefly to stretch and restock. We filled our cooler with ice and extra special picnic food and aimed the VW toward St. Louis.

On the way to St. Louis we saw sign after sign leading us to the Meramac Caverns [Hideout of Jesse James.] Should we or shouldn't we visit these world famous caverns? The signs said they were world famous and this was supposed to be an educational trip so we decided to stop. The kids would be short changed if they hadn't seen Jesse Jame's hideout. The caverns were near the town of Rolla Missouri. We weren't far from Rolla so we decided to stop there for lunch and a much needed break. While we were there we would visit the Meramac Caverns. When we got there we spread out our Indian-looking blanket in a pleasant mosquito infested area and slapped our way through lunch. That done we entered the world famous caverns. The moment we walked into the cavern Tommy panicked. The darkness and the formations of stagnites and stalactites really set him off. Maybe it was the lights reflecting around the cave or the size of the cavern itself. Whatever, its cause, the echo of his screaming made observing this natural wonder a bit difficult. There was no turning back however. I held Tom and reassured him that if he was to fall into a bottomless pit that he would not be alone, Daddy would go with him. Meanwhile Mimi had Carlton and we both told Colleen it was a matter of life and death that she didn't pass the nice lady guide who was leading our tour. In time Tommy calmed down and we did see the wonderful formations and secret rooms where outlaws had stashed their ill-gotten goods and artillery. The world famous cavern tour lasted an hour and then we were again outside in the brilliant sunlit Ozark Mountains. We again spread out our Indian-looking blanket for a dessert picnic and enjoyed the beautiful tree-filled, color-filled, sun-filled park that we found ourselves in on this the third day of our fun-filled family cross country adventure.

When we finished our dessert I loaded up the bug while Mimi and the kids explored the surroundings. When they returned we got them all cleaned up and were again on our way. There were no bottles in sight; the kids were content so the trip to St. Louis looked like a piece of cake. Everything was beautiful! A beautiful wife, beautiful kids, a beautiful car and a beautiful place to drive. As cars passed us we noticed that the people in them were pointing at us. I thought the kids were making faces at them so

I didn't give it a second thought. I thought they were probably just jealous. When a huge truck honked at me and pointed I thought maybe it wasn't jealousy after all, maybe something was wrong. I pulled off the highway and sure enough something was wrong. When I had loaded up the car at the Merrimac Caverns I had thrown our Indian-looking blanket on the luggage carrier and forgotten about it. It in turn had in somehow managed to flutter over the rear of the VW and onto the engine cover where it had caught on fire. Fortunately I got to it before any real damage had occurred. The paint around the motor area of the car had blistered, other than that everything was still in running order. Our Indian-looking blanket was little more than Indian-looking ash. Sadly and with great ceremony we tossed the little bit that was left away. I checked our load carefully and gingerly hit the road again. As we were leaving Colleen was heard to sadly say "Bye Bye blanket". I looked back at Tommy, Colleen and Carlton thankful that nothing had happened to them and was pleased but alarmed to see them all contentedly sucking on a bottle. To this day I wonder where that third bottle had been, who had found it and what possibly could have been in it.

We headed in a northeasterly direction toward St. Louis. It was late afternoon and the countryside was green and very much alive. We were much more aware of each other and the kids after our close call. We decided it would be good to travel a few more hours than stop for dinner and a motel for a good night's sleep. With good food and ample rest we could easily make it to Chicago the following day. Chicago was the home of my aunt and all my cousins, we knew if we made it there we could relax for an evening of good family company and relief from traveling with Kidsaphoebia. But that would be tomorrow, this was today. After driving for a couple of fairly quiet hours, we came to a small town within striking distance of St. Louis. This town was called Sullivan Missouri. Being Irish we figured this had to be our kind of town. We found still another older motel where we cleaned up and got ourselves ready for a night on the town. As fate would have it Colleen and Tommy fell sound asleep while we were getting Carlton organized. We had a dilemma. Should we wake the kids up and go out to dinner or should I go out and see if I could find a place that had something that I could take back to the motel. Mc Donalds hadn't been invented yet and small towns were not rich in fast foods at that time. After much debate, listing pros and cons of waking or not waking the kids, Mimi and I decided to wake them up and go out to dinner, knowing that the family that eats together might possibly sleep through the night together especially if the kids hadn't had naps.

We found a small diner near our motel and graced them with our business. The poor waitress saw what she had as customers and quickly rattled off the special of the day, hot chili with corn bread! We really weren't interested in hot chili and corn bread so we asked for two menus. We ordered grilled cheese sandwiches for the kids and chicken fried steaks for Mimi and me. Colleen and Tom were more asleep than awake so they didn't eat with much gusto. Carlton on the other hand was wide awake and eating anything he could get his hands on. He helped himself to part of his brother and sister's grilled cheese sandwiches. He got a handful of my mashed potatoes and even managed to get Mimi's chicken fried steak off of her fork while it was on the way to her mouth. At this point in time we didn't really worry about the devastation that was surrounding our table. We merely smiled at the customers that seemed to be staring in our direction. We calmly finished our meal, did what little we could to straighten up the mess and returned to our motel for a quick cleanup in preparation for an evening stroll in downtown Sullivan.

Sullivan was no Crestline and Crestline was not much to begin with. Besides our diner, there was a drug store, a small A&P grocery store, a gas station and garage, a couple of bars, a movie theatre and a few other stores that met most of the needs of the people of Sullivan. While Mimi and I window shopped, the kids walked around searching for hidden treasures on the sidewalk and in the gutters. We wandered around Sullivan for about an hour and then returned to our motel for a much needed good night's rest. Fortunately the kids were pretty much worn out so sleep did come. For the first time on our journey a good night's rest was had by all.

We were up at the crack of dawn and on the road as the sun came up. We had decided the night before to have breakfast in St Louis. We reloaded the car. Well rested we took off very optimistically. We were ready for St. Louis and Chicago. Were St. Louis and Chicago ready for us?

After a restful night in Sullivan we were ready for a pleasant trip to Chicago via St. Louis. We arrived in the outskirts of St. Louis in time for a sumptuous breakfast. Instead of chancing a restaurant or diner we decided it would be best if we found a quiet park with a picnic table where we could enjoy our bowls of dry cereal and stale bread. After a calm breakfast with only miner spillage we were back in our VW prison for our trip to and through St. Louis. In to outskirts of St. Luis our three children were weaned off their bottles. All of our reading of various parenting books had made us realize that in order for children to develop a healthy ability to detach the weaning process needed to be slow and loving. As we gathered our three colorful bottles hoping the kids would suck them all the way to Chicago we realized they sounded and felt like they were full of oatmeal. The milk had spoiled. It was then that our children were weaned. The way we looked at it, it was better they had detachment issues later in life than to throw up all over the back seat. We deposited the bottles and the remains of our breakfast into the nearest trash can and we were off to the big city of St Louis.

In St. Louis we pointed out what we thought would be significant places of interest. Museums, old buildings and statues didn't peak their interest. One place that I thought might be worth their while was Stan Musial's restaurant. I'd seen Stan Musial play against the New York Giants and I was really impressed with his cat like batting stance and his ability to hit baseballs. I felt the kids would never forget seeing his restaurant. We also showed them the Gateway Arch that welcomed visitors to the city when they came in over the Mississippi River. Mimi was able to kill two birds with one stone by showing them the Arch and the Mississippi in one look. We were both sure the kids were impressed because we heard them mumbling incoherently due to their going cold turkey from their comforting white, blue, and pink bottles.

We crossed the Mississippi and were traveling on a major highway that would take us all the way to the windy city. The trouble now was the wind was blowing against us. The poor old VW with the luggage on top was chugging along more slowly than all the other vehicles heading north. Even the big semi- trucks were passing us up. The kids were signaling them to blow their horns as they passed. Many of them did which was not music to my ears and almost blew our VW off the road. I finally wised up and got behind one of the big rigs and used his draft to move along at a much faster clip. I only hoped the truck driver was going to Chicago.

We stopped in Springfield for another picnic lunch and then made good time through Bloomington following the draft of another big truck. We entered Chicago over a maze of bridges, barges and railroad tracks. All the movement of trains, barges, trucks and cars kept Carlton, Colleen and Tommy focused and content for many miles as Chicago became a reality. I had been in Chicago once, back in 1948, so I didn't have a clue as to where I was. I knew where I wanted to be but I had no idea where I was.

In 1964 the country was beginning to realize that racial prejudice was alive and well. California had its problems but nothing like the South or the big cities of the Midwest and the East Coast. Chicago was racially divided when we arrived. Naturally we ended up on the south side of the city which was supposedly the wrong place to be. I needed gas and directions but I didn't want to stop for fear some black man would shoot us and take our VW, luggage and possibly the kids. If I didn't take a chance and ask someone, I knew we would probably be in south Chicago for the rest of our lives. I could visualize dying in a VW bug with my wife and three kids. I did take a chance and pulled into a gas station. The gas station attendant was a huge black man that scared us half to death. When I asked him for directions he asked me where we were from. When I told him we were from southern California, he brightened right up and told me he had lived in Los Angeles for ten years. He said he couldn't wait to get out of there and back to Chicago because those Californians scared him to death. We shared the good and the bad about Los Angeles. He drew out directions on a map and told us to enjoy God's country, Chicago. So much for our paranoia. We followed his map and arrived at my Aunt's house in time for dinner.

There's no place like home. My Aunt Gert's house felt like home to five weary travelers. We were greeted by my four cousins who came from all over the area to see their cousin. Our families don't see much of each other so when a cousin comes to town, be it in California or Chicago, it's time for a celebration. The first thing they did was inspect our traveling arrangements. They were overawed at how dumb we really were. The back seat was a mess; Mimi's front seating area contained a small cooler while the back of the car was charbroiled around the motor. They looked with disbelief as we showed them the intricate arrangements we had made for our journey. They said they too would like to drive across country in a VW bug someday, but not right then. I told them when they were ready they could have ours as we might not ever want to see it again.

They took us into their home which was two floors of a large apartment building they owned on Glenwood Avenue. They showed us to the bathroom encouraging us to clean up for dinner. After a thorough scrubbing we came back to the group. They hardly recognized us in our new state of cleanliness. Dinner was a typical family meal, everyone talking at once. It was good just being able to talk to adults for a change. Even the kids enjoyed the change of scenery and for once didn't make a mess of things. We talked into the night. That night we slept in comfortable beds, a perfect ending for the best day of our cross country journey. When we said goodbye to our cousins they offered us their condolences as we were returning to our VW snake pit.

Bright and early the next morning we were ready for the final run to Buffalo. After our first real breakfast since leaving California and with ample supplies courtesy of my aunt, we leaped into the bug and were on our way. There's not a whole lot to see when you travel from Chicago to Buffalo. Indiana is flat, the roads are straight and the scenery as far as we were concerned was boring. Fortunately the wind was with us as we headed east. We were determined to make it to Buffalo by late evening. The one place in Indiana that caught our attention was Notre Dame and the golden dome that you could see for miles. Mimi and I had always wanted to visit the Notre Dame campus but this was not the time. We looked at that beautiful golden dome and imagined what the rest of the university must have looked like. When we saw Lake Erie we knew we were in the home stretch because Buffalo is on Lake Erie and Mimi used to visit her aunt who had a summer home on the lake. Lake Erie is one big lake so we knew we still had a long way to go.

We stopped for the lunch near Toledo. After eating the sandwiches my aunt had prepared for us we boarded our bug and drove north to Cleveland which was in striking distance of Buffalo. It wasn't long before we were driving along the Cleveland lakefront. Mimi had an aunt in Cleveland who wasn't home at the time so there was no reason to stop in Cleveland. We'd been driving a long time so once we were past the city we stopped and let the kids run off some of their pent up energy. Mimi and I spent the time trying to straighten out our backs and legs while dreaming of the day we'd be out of that infernal automobile. Back in the car and off we were to Pennsylvania.

The North western corner of Pennsylvania is beautiful part of the state. It is covered with dense woods that are especially vibrant in early June. Driving is easy when you're surrounded such beauty. There were stretches where you could see the lake on one side and the thick woods on the other. Even when you're tired, scenery like that kept you alert because you didn't want to miss a thing. We went by many pleasant farms, saw horses, cattle and numerous deer. On a sunny June afternoon, driving a VW bug with a wife and three kids mashed in the back seat, Northwestern Pennsylvania was the place to be.

We were breezing along and I was exhausted. I figured it was near seven o'clock at night because it was what seven o'clock was like in California. When I looked at my watch I realized it was almost ten o'clock and we still had quite a ways to go. What a surprise for Mimi's Mom and Dad when they would be awakened after one o'clock in the morning. By now the kids were sleeping so it was Mimi's job to keep me awake for the last few hours of our epic voyage. She did a good job by going over all the plans she had for the time we would be visiting her old hometown. The sun had gone down. Slowly but surely we started to drive by places that Mimi remembered from before we were married. Before long a sign saying "Buffalo 10 miles" came into view. Lancaster wasn't much farther than that so the adrenaline began to take over. Mimi began pointing out all the ice cream stores. According to her the best ice cream in the world could *only* be found in Buffalo, along with the best tomatoes, the best hot dogs, the *only* Beef on Wick sandwiches worth eating and beer. She pointed out the local bars and hangouts. We passed her school, the railroad tracks, the water company and finally we were on her street. Livingston Street never looked better. We found her driveway, turned in, parked on the back lawn and fell out of our capsule. We made it!

There was no one up to greet us. We took care of that by beating on the door and waking up the whole neighborhood. The noise added a festive note to our arrival. Mimi's mom and dad were overjoyed at seeing their daughter and grandchildren. They looked at the VW and shook their heads and held their noses for it really did send forth an odor after five days of leaky diapers. We didn't get to bed right away for there was a lot to talk about. It was well after three when exhaustion finally set in.

The summer went by quickly. California was three thousand miles away. We had to get back, as teachers were expected to be back by the time school started. We made preparations for the return trip. The back seat was again converted to a playpen for the kids. The front end of the VW was packed full of our luggage. Food and necessities were placed on the floor under the playpen. The luggage rack on top of the car was empty so there would be no wind resistance. Just as we were taking off Mimi's dad presented us with a copper wash tub he had found in the woods. Since we had nothing on the luggage rack it would fit quite easily. I nodded in disbelief. It was just what we needed, for what I don't know, but we got it on the luggage rack and were finally ready. Like the pioneers before us, we headed west singing California here we come.

Here we were, Mimi and I in the front seat, Carlton, Colleen and Tommy, bigger now because of Gramma's cooking, enjoying the playpen, a few toys and no bottles. After about two hours on the road, Mimi asked how much longer do we have to endure this punishment. We hadn't even made it to Cleveland. I drove as far as I could as I wanted to get back to California as fast as I could. The only problem was the copper bath tub. It stuck up so high that it served as a wind barrier and the poor VW wouldn't go over fifty miles per hour. At that rate it was going to take at least sixty hours to make it to Crestline. We could do nothing to speed up the trip. Giving up the copper bathtub was out of the question because Mimi had fallen in love with it. So we plodded onward toward Chicago and my Aunt Gertrude's house.

We made it to my Aunt's house in two very slow days. The family was beginning to deteriorate. Tommy, who was two was crying all the time, Colleen wanted to go back and play with her cousins, Carlton was constantly in need of clean diapers and Mimi wanted to commit suicide. By the time we reached Chicago the trip was proving to be a disaster. What had we been thinking when we decided to drive cross country and back in a shoebox? It was good to be out of that miserable VW. We spent a comfortable night at my aunt's house. At breakfast we discussed the journey ahead. My cousins suggested that I get a job in Chicago and give up the trip home. Cooler heads prevailed. It was decided that the best thing we could do was lighten the load. To do so, we'd send Mimi and Tommy back on an airplane. Carlton, Colleen and I would continue our westward trek together as a happy threesome.

It was raining when we left Chicago. Undaunted, we headed back to California, a little bit lighter, but still carrying a copper bathtub on top of our VW bug. The rain was incessant. Fortunately, the windshield wipers were still working so onward ever onward we went retracing our tracks on Route 66. I drove twelve hours each day. I only stopped to change diapers, buy hotdogs and stretch. We'd find a motel each night, sleep, wake up, eat cold cereal, get back in our cage and head west. People would pass by me and look at me with strange expressions seeming to wonder what was going on with that guy with the two little kids and a copper bath tub and where could he possibly be going? I paid no attention to their puzzled looks and kept on plodding through Texas, Oklahoma, New Mexico, until we finally made it to Arizona only one state away from home.

As I look back the whole trip back to California was a blur of occasional sun and incessant rain. As we entered Arizona, I found a little place where I could buy hamburgers to go. I bought three good looking hamburgers and thought we could find a nice place for a picnic down the road. After we drove about a mile, the rains came. I figured the storm would pass and then we would have our picnic. The storm never let up. Our good looking hamburgers were getting cold, our milk was getting warm and there was no end in sight with the rain.

As we were approaching the border of California, the rain finally stopped but I could not find a picnic area. I did however find a gas station with a lonely bench against the station wall. We sat on that lonely bench and ate the cold, sad looking hamburgers that I had bought five hours earlier.

Carlton and Colleen were so hungry they didn't even notice how bad the food really was.

We entered California at Needles. I stopped at the first California store I could find and bought a six pack to celebrate being back on our own turf, even though we were still at least six hours from home. It was early evening so I figured I'd go for it. I got the VW back on the freeway and headed home. We passed through the inspection station where the ranger took one look at us, shook his head and didn't even ask if we had any fruit or produce. He just waved us through. It was then that I popped open a beer and joyfully celebrated the last two hundred miles of our New York trip. Time went very slowly as night turned into morning. We made it to our turn off and headed up the mountain toward Crestline. We finally made it to our house. It was three o'clock in the morning. Fortunately, my eyes were still open. Carlton was asleep and Colleen was wide awake. When we pulled into the driveway and stopped, Colleen jumped out of the car, ran into the house and turned on the TV. I carried Carlton in and Mimi sleepily greeted the long lost travelers. We finally got the TV off and the kids in bed. I promptly passed out on our bed. The VW with the Copper bath tub on top sat in our driveway for the next two days before we could even approach it again. The New York trip had finally come to a dead end.

SCHOOL OF HOPE

Carlton right about the time he went to The School of Hope

Since President Gerald Ford signed Public Law 94-142 into law, every child in the United States has been entitled to an education. Before that time children could be restricted from school for many reasons. Carlton was denied access to public school because he was severely handicapped and he wasn't toilet trained. Restrictions like these kept children like Carlton at home and made a difficult situation worse for their parents.

Some private schools were established for these children. Some were started by the Association for Retarded Children, some by parents and some by public schools. The demand far outweighed the supply.

There was no school for children with special needs in the San Bernardino Mountains. Mountain schools were dependent on the county of San Bernardino for their support services. The parents of the eight or ten retarded youngsters living in the Rim of the World School District petitioned the County to begin a special class within the school district in 1964. The County agreed to furnish a teacher. The Methodist Church in Lake Arrowhead agreed to rent classroom space. Carlton was enrolled in the inaugural class. Every morning a county van, driven by the classroom aid would pick Carlton up and transport him to his new school. Carlton would spend five hours each day learning new skills and then be returned home early each afternoon. Mimi and I were very pleased. Carlton would learn new skills, and Mimi would be able to spend some time with Colleen and Tommy.

Our excitement was short lived. Before the first week was over the driver who drove Carlton each day said it was impossible for her to deal with Carlton and the other children. Between watching the children and watching the curving mountain roads the situation was unsafe. If Carlton was to attend school, Mimi and I would have to get him there. Mimi was pregnant with our fourth child. I was teaching. Transporting Carlton fifteen miles round trip to Lake Arrowhead was impossible.

With no transportation available, we had to withdraw Carlton from the school. Our hopes again crashed down on us. His teacher told us later that the school was not set up for children like Carlton in the first place. She felt it would have been a waste of his time and hers to have him in school. This was not a good start for Carlton in his quest for an education.

A year or so later we learned of a school in San Bernardino, the School of Hope, established by the Association for Retarded Children for retarded persons of all ages. Carlton was welcome to attend if we could get him there but no transportation was available. In our search for a way to get him to the school, we met two other families with severely handicapped children. The parents of the other two children agreed to transport the children down and back two days each if Mimi could manage the trip one day a week. With the help of my mother, Mimi was able to take her turn driving the children to school. We enrolled Carlton in the School of Hope.

For Mimi and the three children, Carlton, Jimmy and Kathy it was a nerve racking fifteen mile drive down a two lane curving mountain road to the School of Hope. To make matters worse the County was widening the road through the mountain. Some days the trip took an hour and a half one way because of construction, but it was well worth it. School of Hope accepted Carlton as he was. The teachers worked with him, developing the basic skills of dressing, eating and toilet training.

The School of Hope lived up to its name. It gave us hope. Carlton was enrolled in the infant and preschool program. We quickly saw definite improvement in his behavior. His first teacher was an exceptional person except for one major flaw, she was an alcoholic. She had her drinking under control most of the time but occasionally she arrived at school a little tipsy, finally the school had to let her go. Fortunately she was replaced by another caring, insightful teacher, Mrs. Strange.

There were no requirements for teachers in schools like the School of Hope. They were hired according to the principal's criteria. Those employed were usually caring people who had raised children of their own. They seemed to thoroughly enjoy working with their handicapped students. They weren't paid much for their incredible effort. They had no models. They became the model when schooling was mandated. There were no method courses or teacher training programs available to them, so they developed materials and programs geared to each child's particular need. They were true pioneers in working with the severely handicapped.

Mrs. Strange loved Carlton. She worked hard to unlock the potential hidden behind his veil of silence. Undaunted by his lack of understanding, she devised ways to help him learn some basic skills. She had him sorting objects by size, shape and color.

One skill Carlton did have was the ability to spit up at will the food he had eaten. Mimi and I tried everything we could think of to break him of the habit. We held him, played with him, scolded him, held his hands so he couldn't make himself regurgitate, but nothing seemed to stop it. Mrs. Strange stopped it with a small spray bottle of water that she kept handy, when Carlton spit up, she sprayed his face. Within a week she had stopped his spitting up during the school day. The method was effective at home as long as we remembered where the bottle was or where Carlton was. We learned that consistency was the key to Carlton's progress. Sometimes consistency was hard to come by in a house with the likes of Colleen, Tommy and Alicia.

Now we are six. The family is complete. I am holding Tommy and Carlton. Mimi is holding Alicia. Colleen is sitting down.

Jimmy and Kathy were higher functioning than Carlton. Jimmy had the ability to remember people's names. When someone came to visit his mother or father, he greeted them by name even if they hadn't been there for over a year. As they were approaching the school one morning, Jimmy tapped Mimi on the shoulder. "Here we are again," he said. "Where Jim?" Mimi asked. Laughing, Jim said, "At the School of the Hopeless". Jimmy knew what he was saying.

That day Mimi went in to visit Mrs. Strange. Unfortunately she wasn't there. She was home recuperating from being bitten by Carlton. Carlton had swallowed a weed and was choking. Mrs. Strange reached into his mouth to extract it. Carlton tried to devour her hand. When she did get her finger out, the skin had been broken and it was badly bruised. After a tetanus shot and a few days of healing, she was able to return. Later she told Mimi that Carlton had taught her a lesson and she would be a better teacher because of it. With teachers like Mrs. Strange, Carlton was in good hands as long as they were kept out of his mouth.

Carlton remained at the School of Hope for two years. Friends living near us took him to school and back after Alicia was born. He was happy there. He did projects with clay and finger paints. He was in Christmas plays, patriotic plays and Easter Pageants. He was part of something, a member of a group.

Sometimes it's hard for grandfathers and grandmothers and close family members to accept the reality of a retarded child. Our family was different. They received Carlton with open arms. My dad loved Carlton and often wrote stories about him. He was enamored with the School of Hope and the loving people that worked there. After going to a School of Hope Christmas show he had this to say:

> "An exciting and important event took place in the Smith family during the holidays. One of my grandsons made his debut in the American Theatre. It wasn't much of a part. He didn't have any lines to speak, but then that didn't matter; he hasn't said a word since he was born some seven years ago. Charley, his real name is Carlton, but I call him Charley because he seems to like it- is what is mentioned in public print as a Retarded Child. It's more or less a shocking combination of words to some people and makes them feel guilty and embarrassed. It depends on the way you look at it. For my money most of us grown ups are retarded if you look at the shape we've put the world in these days. It really doesn't matter much to Charley how you label him. He goes on in his own little way in his own enchanted little world, seeing things as he sees them. And it must be a much more pleasant view he gets than we do, for he never beefs, never worries, never demands this or that He simply takes each day and what it contains as it comes and lives it in his own silent, quiet little way, without any complaints and waits for the next day to bob along. Last fall his parents, my son

Carl and his wife Mimi, took him down the hill and entered him in a miraculous school, whose staff have a wonderful God given gift--a talent for loving the kind of kids Charley is and making them tick. They have that something extra that dedicated people have which enables them to understand them and break through the veil that some quirk of fate has wrapped them in. You can have Oxford and Harvard and Yale even that great institution up at Berkeley. Give me the School of Hope, that's the name of Charley's Alma Mater. There is something there, as the name suggests, that few institutions of learning possess, Hope. In as much as Charley's ma and pa both teach in Crestline the daily trip down loomed up as almost impossible, so they set up a cry for help. They came up with three prizes, Laurie Bogart, Kathy O'Neill and a gentleman named Costillo. Every day Laurie and Kathy buzz by Carl's house in their bug, bundle Charley up and tote him down to the School of Hope. Every afternoon Mr. Costillo who works below brings him back up. In the short time he has been there, Charley has made great strides. So much so that he won a part in the annual Christmas play. It wasn't a star part; Charley was chosen to play an ornament. His duty was to stand beneath the tree and add to its splendor and beauty. He performed his role perfectly. His smile outshone the lights of the tree. No graduate of any Actors Workshop or method actor could have improved on it in any way. He did his best, Angels can do no more".

Carlton at 7 months his first Christmas

The School of Hope years were two of the best years for Carlton and the Smith family. It was five years from the time he left the School of Hope until he was able to attend another school program.

Mimi and I the same year (1959) with my mom and dad

REGIONAL CENTER (THE SUITS)

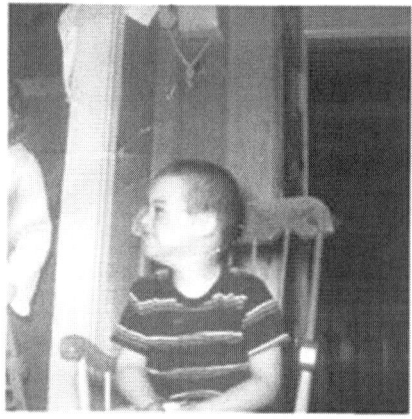

Carlton at 6 in his rocking chair

While Carlton was going to the School of Hope we heard about a new approach to dealing with severely handicapped children, the multi-disciplinary approach to mental retardation. We'd read about it and we had seen Dr. Richard Koch on TV discussing this new method. Dr. Koch was a renowned authority on Down's syndrome children. He was on the staff at UCLA and the leading consultant on retardation to the State of California. We were pleased to learn that research was being done to help the Carltons of this world. We hoped that this new approach might be beneficial for all of them.

Under the auspices of the State of California, Dr. Koch was going to begin a training program for this new approach in San Bernardino. In time, the State would set up a system that would better serve its retarded citizens.

In l966, the Association for Retarded Children (ARC) was a force to be reckoned with. The State was trying to come up with a service network that would make sense out of its chaotic mental health situation. There was a three year waiting list for State Hospital placement. Most patients in State hospitals survived for no more than three years. Those that did were put in the infamous back rooms and cared for as babies for the rest of their lives. It was common practice to place a retarded child as far away as possible from the parents' home. The rule of thumb was, "out of sight out of mind".

Taking these factors into consideration, and hearing from more and more parents of retarded children, the state, under the direction of Dr. Koch, began to set up a service system of regional centers for the retarded, central points in various areas of California, where parents of a retarded child could go for help. There, their child would be assessed, programs would be made available, and professionals would be able to help the parents keep their child at home. If raising a son or daughter at home was impossible, suitable placement would be found to meet the child's needs. It was a new concept and in time would develop into what we know today as The Regional Centers for the Developmentally Disabled. Mimi and I were confident that this multidiscipline approach would be beneficial, as well as educational for families with retarded children.

When we became involved with The Regional Center System, it was in its infancy. Carlton had just turned six, long since he was an easy baby, now he was a handful. He had been asked to leave his school in Lake Arrowhead. He was doing all right at The School of Hope in San Bernardino, but the fourteen mile trip to and from school was taking its toll on Mimi and our family. We had asked the county for help but nothing was available. There was a public school in Bloomington that served the needs of some retarded children. It was run by the Bloomington School District as an experimental program; however it was full and too far away to help us.

One day we received a letter from San Bernardino County telling us of a new regional center program that the State was considering for the County. There was going to be a training program for potential regional center leaders. Our family had been selected to participate in a training program for potential regional center leaders. Dr. Koch, himself, would be heading the training team.

We readily agreed to take part. Finally help was on the way. We were ecstatic. We knew that with a little help, Carlton could manage and so could we. We received a questionnaire in the mail which we filled out and sent back to the County office. Before long we received a notice saying we would be interviewed at the San Bernardino County Administration Building the following week. We were thrilled. For once something positive seemed to be happening.

We didn't know what to expect but we were excited about the prospects of a school or program that would meet Carlton's and our needs. We didn't know what our needs were but we knew we definitely had some. Maybe, just maybe, these experts from the State would have some answers that would make our situation more tenable.

The day arrived for our appointment. We were nervous but hopeful. We dressed Carlton in his sharpest outfit. Mimi and I shared our anxieties and our hopes as we drove down the hill towards San Bernardino and the county administration building.

A woman, who said she was a social worker, led us to a small room with three chairs in it. She told us that the first part of the procedure would be a physical examination of Carlton. She asked us to undress him to hurry things along. As we were undressing him, I looked at Mimi and Carlton and felt isolated. It was a very uncomfortable situation. I said to Mimi, "They've put us in jail". We laughed but in our hearts we felt helpless.

Finally it was time to take Carlton for his physical. Instead of a small conference with two or three professionals as we had expected, we were led into a large room. At least ten important looking people sat at two fold up tables, placed end to end. They were shuffling through stacks of papers. Surrounding the table on all sides were temporary bleachers. Everything in the room looked like an afterthought, last minute bleachers, last minute furniture and last minute people.

The stands were filled with social workers, psychologists, doctors and other professionals, who were learning the process of forming a Regional Center. It reminded me of my high school gymnasium when we had a boxing match. There were two seats at the table for Mimi and me. Carlton could sit on one of our laps. The only person we recognized was Dr. Koch because he had been on T. V. and was involved with The School of Hope.

Without any introductions, he started to examine Carlton. We couldn't believe what was happening to us and our child. Here he was naked and frightened in front of a large audience. He looked so frail, his small body shaking and a look of terror in his eyes, Dr. Koch poked and listened, manipulated his arms and legs, took his blood pressure and felt him all over for any abnormalities. Carlton didn't cry but Mimi and I could tell by the hurt expression on his face that he was apprehensive and scared. It seemed to us that the consensus of the group was that retarded children had no feelings and weren't even aware of the world around them.

When Dr. Koch was finished with Carlton, we were dismissed and told we could take him back to our cubicle and dress him. We stared at each other in complete dismay. No one had told us what to expect. No one had told us who would be involved with Carlton or us. There were no introductions of the people at the table. No one had offered us the least bit of hospitality. And now we found ourselves back in a little cubicle no bigger than a confessional, putting our son's clothes back on. We didn't even have a table. He was lying on a chair. We knew he was probably scared to death because we certainly were.

After about twenty minutes the social worker returned and told us she had to take Carlton back for his mental assessment. She assured us that it wouldn't be too long before she'd bring him back. When she returned, she said he had done just fine and we'd be called out in a little while. Mimi looked at me and asked if I had any idea of what "just fine" meant. We knew Carlton couldn't read, write or understand directions. He couldn't match shapes or determine colors or identify anything so how could he do "just fine"? We were having second thoughts about this whole affair but there seemed to be no escape. We waited.

About forty five minutes later we were escorted back to the arena. I knew then how the martyrs felt when they were lead into the lions' den. Dr. Koch began explaining the results of Carlton's physical exam. While he was doing this he kept spinning around so that everyone in the bleachers could see and hear him. There were many knowing professional nods as he spoke. The only three people in the place he ignored were Mimi, Carlton and me.

When he was done, he turned the floor over to one of his colleagues, probably a psychiatrist, who then went off in another direction describing another phase of Carlton's life. He was able to inform us that Carlton had an IQ of 3. Being a teacher I knew IQ scores had a tolerance of plus or minus ten points. I only hoped Carlton's score was on the positive side.

When he finished, the people at the table asked us if we had any questions. We had none. We were speechless. We had been struck mute. Seeing we had no questions, another person took the floor and began speaking directly to us. He spoke in glowing terms of how wonderful things were "out there". He went on to tell us that everyone "out there" was happy and healthy and living life to its fullest. He told us we'd all be better off when Carlton was "out there". I could control myself no longer. I couldn't imagine any place other than heaven that could be as beautiful and life giving as "out there", so I asked him just where "out there" was. He looked at me with a kind of holier than thou expression and gently confided to me that "out there" was Pacific State Hospital.

I'd heard about state hospitals and his "out there" and what I'd heard just didn't mesh. The only reply I could mutter was "oh". We realized that they had decided that Carlton must leave our home to spend his life in an institution. We were fuming inside. They asked us if we had any more questions. We told them we weren't sure if we did or not. Then we were led back to our confessional.

We looked at each other. Mimi didn't seem to know what had just happened so she asked me. I assured her I didn't know either. We just sat there and awaited our fate and the fate of Carlton. The social worker came back and escorted us to the arena again. The experts at the table thanked us for our participation. They wished us good luck and told us we'd be hearing from them in the near future. The people in the grandstand applauded and we were guided to the door.

As we were walking to our car, I told Mimi we must have been pretty good to get all that applause. We drove to a restaurant nearby and tried to drown our sorrows with ice cream sundaes. On the way home we talked about the treatment we had received. We talked about all those experts at the table. We wondered if they really recognized Carlton and his parents as being human. We knew about as much then as we did before we went down the hill earlier that morning. We had hoped to find help for ourselves and our family. Instead they wanted to take Carlton away from us. We had been tossed into the lions' den and torn apart by the lions. We seriously questioned this multidisciplinary approach to mental retardation. It had been a bad day.

PLACEMENT

Pacific State Hospital

Mimi and I had been married for eight years. We had four children. In the last year Mimi had developed diabetes. We were struggling to keep things together. We were receiving no help for Carlton. When we finally thought we were going to get some relief through this multidisciplinary approach, we only found more disappointment. We waited for some word from the state, the county, Dr. Koch and his Regional Center Program or anyone who might be able to give us some guidance.

About a month after our interview in San Bernardino, we received a letter asking if we might be interested in respite care for our son which gave families with severely handicapped children a break for a specific period of time. It also was a preparation for the day when the family might find it necessary to place their child permanently.

There was an opening at Pacific State Hospital for six weeks of respite care during the summer. We replied that we would like to consider their offer. We hadn't had any time for ourselves for more than seven years. We'd been so involved with Carlton during that time that we couldn't comprehend even a week without him. Six weeks with Colleen, Tommy and Alicia sounded too good to be true. We had our small trailer and we had the time. We could have a family vacation.

It wasn't easy placing Carlton for the summer. We had visited Pacific State Hospital and did not like what we saw. There were thirty or more retarded children in each barn like dormitory. Each bed was netted over so the child couldn't climb out. It was more like a warehouse for handicapped children than the home-like facility we had hoped for. Knowing that it would only last six weeks, we decided to go ahead with the placement.

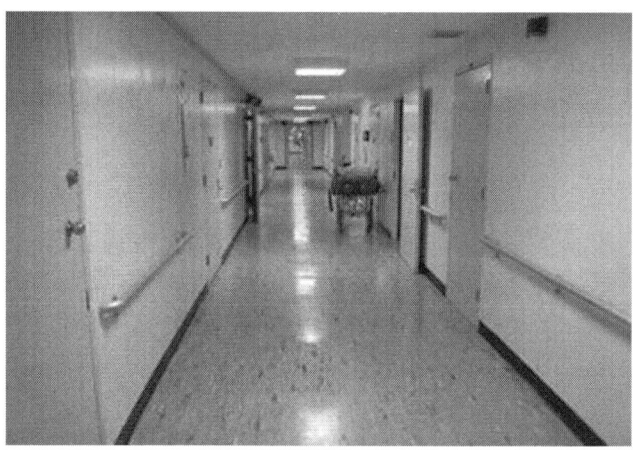

Pacific State hospital. These long halls lead to rooms where there were 30 beds with a child in each bed

Our trailer trip to New York to visit Mimi's parents was an eye opener. We hadn't realized the amount of time that Carlton required. We also realized how little we knew our own children, Colleen, Tommy and Alicia. We explored the country, visited friends and camped out in Mimi's sister's back yard. Our kids were able to play with their many cousins. We did things that we could never do before. We knew, before the trip was over, that we would eventually have to find a suitable situation for Carlton.

When we went down to Pacific State Hospital to pick up Carlton, he seemed happy to see us and to return to his home in Crestline. The family was whole again. We had enjoyed our vacation, but having Carlton home filled a void. He had been missed.

When we picked him up, he just wasn't himself. Carlton looked pale and seemed to have lost some weight. We discovered he had a full blown case of diarrhea. Our doctor prescribed everything from medication to special diets. Nothing worked. The doctor admitted he hadn't a clue to what was ailing our son. We bathed him four or five times a day. He took all of our time and we were getting nowhere.

Finally our doctor had him admitted to the hospital for five days of testing and medication. He was sent home after five days. When he got home, we saw no improvement whatsoever. The situation persisted. My Mother came over to relieve Mimi during the day. I came home from school and took over until we put Carlton to bed. This went on for three or four months. After four months a friend of ours, who was into health foods, suggested we try acidophilus enriched milk. She said it would build up bacteria in Carlton's system and help him digest his food. We were willing to try anything.

We started giving Carlton the acidophilus enriched milk and soon saw a marked improvement. We were amazed. Not one of the many doctors who had consulted with us had mentioned acidophilus. We had to hear it from a "health nut". Within three weeks Carlton was cured and we were able to get back to a normal routine. His illness had taken a toll on us. My mother's daily assistance was the only reason we were able to make it through an almost impossible situation. We knew we couldn't handle our situation much longer.

Pacific State Hospital had a long mixed history of both good and bad. It sat on 300 acres of prime land and was in operation for over 80 years. In the end it boasted a campground, a soda shop, and an equestrian complex. It was closed in 2011 and is now reported to be haunted and hosts a haunted house every Halloween. I can't help but laugh at the thought of past residents haunting the halls and pulling hijinks. With my experience it does not seem scary at all. The scary part is long past and it was for the living.

The following summer we received word that a new facility for the retarded was going to open in Bloomington which was about twenty five miles from our home in Crestline. Mimi and I drove to Bloomington for a tour of this facility, Bloomington Convalescent Center. It had its own barber shop, twenty-four hour nursing care and a nice community room. Each room had two beds, a closet, a dresser and a bathroom. The facility was spotless. It even had a play yard. It reminded us of a hospital, but it was still by far the best facility of its kind that we had ever seen. It certainly looked like a possible answer for Carlton.

Mimi and I knew in our hearts that placement for Carlton was inevitable, but we wondered whether this was the right one. We wondered if it would be possible to let Carlton go. If we did decide to place him, how would we deal with our family and friends? We couldn't worry about what they might think. We had to think of our children and ourselves first.

We talked to our social worker often the next few days. We wanted assurances that placing Carlton would not be an irreversible process. We needed to know that we could bring him back home at any time, visit him at any time, and that we'd be informed immediately if he became ill. We were determined to remain his parents even if we were to place him at Bloomington.

Our social worker assured us we would be involved in all decisions involving Carlton. We could take him back at any time and visit as often and whenever we wanted. If we decided to place him in Bloomington, however, we would be asked not to visit him for a three week adjustment period to help Carlton get used to his new situation.

It was now up to us to make this very trying decision. Mimi and I thought about the past, the good times, trips, family adventures, Christmases and happy moments. We thought about the bad times, sicknesses, traveling up and down the hill to school, our other children passing Carlton up, the constant spitting up and the many anxious moments. We thought about the future, no schools, no programs, no playmates for Carlton and no place to find help or understanding. We would have to explain it to Colleen, Tommy and Alicia. Carlton was their brother and they loved him very much.

Carlton on his 11th birthday with his sisters Colleen (left) and Alicia (right) 1970

We prayed for guidance. After much soul searching and hours of talking deep into the night, we knew that we must let Carlton go to Bloomington. We thought about what Dr. Sterling had said a couple of years before, "You'll know when the time is right." We knew the time was now. Bloomington was a beautiful new facility; it seemed to be a friendly place, well equipped to handle Carlton's needs, and it wasn't too far away.

We called our social worker and told her of our decision. The following Tuesday was set for Carlton's placement. That gave us five days to prepare for our son's leaving home.

We told our families and friends of our decision. Some responded with loving understanding, but others put a guilt trip on us and told us we were making a big mistake. One said "We'd regret it for the rest of our lives". No matter what they said, the decision had been made. Mimi and I would have to live with it.

We talked to our children about their brother. We explained how Carlton would always need special care which we would be unable to provide. We assured them that Carlton was still their brother and always would be. He would still be part of the family and come home to spend weekends with us.

We told Colleen and Tom that they would have more time to play with their little sister and Carlton would have many new friends of his own. Then we let them help us get his belongings ready for the move.

Tuesday arrived, and to this day, over fifty years later, we still don't want to think about it. We packed Carlton's clothes that Mimi had carefully marked with his name. We gathered his favorite toys, a stuffed bear, a ball and a noisy banging toy that his Grampa had made him. We took his little rocking chair that he loved to sit in and rock. We dressed him in his nicest clothes and began our lonely trip down the hill to Bloomington.

We were greeted by the owner Mr. Plovis, a middle aged man who didn't seem overly interested in us. He was more interested in getting Carlton moved in. He tried to put us at ease by telling us how happy everyone at Bloomington was. His words fell on deaf ears. Mimi and I could see no happiness in this situation.

He showed us Carlton's new room, and then wisely left us alone. It was antiseptically clean. There was a bed, a closet and a dresser for his clothes. Mr. Plovis said we could arrange Carlton's things any way we wanted them. He suggested that we send Carlton cards and each one would be read to him.

He reminded us of the three week transition period. He encouraged us to call anytime. The staff would fill us in on what was happening. After the three weeks we would be able to bring the family to visit or take Carlton home for a day. He tried to be comforting but we weren't comforted. We straightened out Carlton's room, put his toys where he could get them, placed him in his little rocking chair and left.

We didn't go out to lunch on the way home. We weren't hungry. We felt empty. The trip home was a quiet one. We didn't have much to talk about. We had talked so much those past few days that we were talked out. Our car seemed to get home on its own. I don't remember driving it. My mother was waiting for us when we got home. It was a tearful homecoming. She knew how we felt. She too felt the loneliness and hurt.

When Colleen and Tommy got home from school they didn't seem to notice our pain. They knew we were taking Carlton to his new home that morning but it didn't seem to affect them. Mimi and I thought they'd be crying and upset but we didn't know our own children. They did what little children do. They played, they argued and they watched TV. They didn't mention Carlton.

Slowly, during the following days, we were able to return to some semblance of normal family life. We knew Carlton would be all right. We had our four beautiful children, three at home, one away. We had each other.

Tommy's 11th birthday. Carlton celebrating with us (I am holding him back from the cake). Carlton was everyone's favorite brother....he never talked back!

Soon after Carlton left, Tommy began crying at night and wetting his bed. Carlton had shared the room with him. When we held Tommy and hugged him, we could tell he was unhappy and scared. When he was finally able to talk about it, he asked if we had sent Carlton away because we were mad at him. If so he was going to try and be real good so he could stay home. Carlton was placed at Bloomington. Now Mimi and I realized we had a lot of extra parenting to do with Colleen, Tommy and Alicia.

CARLTON LOST

Carlton on a visit home 1970

Carlton had only been in Bloomington for two months when I received a phone call on a Thursday morning, "Mr. Smith, my name is Alex Plovis. I am the owner of Bloomington Convalescent Home, the facility your son Carlton was living in until two days ago. Would you please call your social worker and ask if your son might come back to my facility?"

I was stunned, what did he mean he was there until two days ago? Where was my son? Why was he moved? It was bad enough having to place our eight year old son into the care of others. Now he had been moved and I wanted to know why Mimi and I were the last ones to find out about it.

I immediately called our social worker whom I had met only once when she came to the house and had us fill out a twenty six page questionnaire about our family and our life history, the first step in the process of getting an out-of-home placement for our son. When I finally got through to her, I asked her what in the world was going on with Carlton. It seems Bloomington Convalescent Home was having some sanitation problems so the state felt it was urgent to move the "clients" to a safer haven. I asked why we weren't notified of this situation. Her reply was the response I have grown accustomed to over these many years, "we didn't want to upset you." After assuring her that she could upset me anytime a major incident happens in my son's life, I asked her "Where is Carlton now?" In her soothing voice she said, "I don't know." Within an hour and a half I had been informed that my son no longer lived where he had been living and the person who was managing his case didn't know where he was "Welcome to the system," I thought to myself. Mimi and I had to find our son.

Which way to turn? If our social worker couldn't help us, who could? We asked our social worker if she could at least direct us to someone who might know of Carlton's whereabouts. She gave us the name of her administrator, a Mr. Pierce, at Pacific State Hospital. We called and were told to leave our name and phone number and he would make it a point to get back to us the following day.

Friday morning passed without a phone call. Late that afternoon Mr. Pierce's secretary called. She told us that they had received our message and would be sure to get back to us first thing Monday morning. I told her that we didn't feel we could wait until Monday to find our son. We wanted action now. She said they wanted to help us, but it would take them at least until Monday to locate Carlton. Mimi and I and our three other children endured a long weekend of worry and confusion. We counted the hours until we would see Carlton again.

Monday finally arrived and with it came a call from Mr. Pierce. In a friendly voice he explained, at great length, how the State looked out for children like Carlton especially when it came to issues of health. That is why Carlton was moved from Bloomington Convalescent Home. Mr. Pierce was pleased that they had acted so quickly and that the individuals who were moved were still in good health. I guess he felt this bit of news would be comforting to us. As usual, "the system" did not want upset parents. He gave us the names and addresses of two facilities where he thought we might find our boy. Mr. Pierce wasn't too sure which one Carlton was placed in because things happened so fast. He was quite sure however, that he'd be in one of them. Regardless, he reassured us, no matter where Carlton was, he was fine and he'd help us find him. Before he hung up he told me in all sincerity, not to worry.

Needless to say Mimi and I were in a state of shock. Even though Carlton had left home, he was still part of our family. We didn't love him any less. He had been out of our home and living at Bloomington Convalescent for six weeks. We had just gone through the worst period of our lives entrusting him to the care of others and now we didn't even know where he was. What could we do? It was urgent that we find Carlton. What would we do when we did find him? In situations like this prayer became our only source of hope. Pray we did.

With map in hand Mimi and I headed down the hill toward Pomona and the two addresses we'd been given. Our first destination was a small fifteen bed facility. We introduced ourselves to the woman in charge and explained our dilemma. She was a very warm and understanding person, sympathetic but unable to help us. She had no new children admitted to her care for over a month.

She took us on a tour of her home and it was easy for us to see the loving care she gave the handicapped children who were placed in her home. We learned from her just how dedicated and loving people who worked with severely handicapped children could be. She gave us hope. We felt that maybe there could be a place for Carlton in a home like this even though it was far from our home in Crestline, but we had to find him first.

At the next home on our list we were greeted by a pleasant middle aged woman, who was the mother of a severely retarded son. She had been determined to keep her son at home so she began taking in others like him. As her family of handicapped children grew so did her house. Her home now had twenty beds in it. Keeping a home like this going had taken a toll on her. Her hair was prematurely grey and she looked tired. She was a very positive person none the less. Yes, she did have a Carlton, a new arrival who just might be our son.

She took us to his room with five cribs in it. She showed us where he slept. His was the only empty bed. She said in her gentle way that he was probably wandering again. All the persons living there were non ambulatory except Carlton so he posed a definite threat as he ambled all over the place. She never knew where he might be. We all searched and finally found him playing in a far off corner. I picked him up. Mimi and I hugged and kissed him. We had found our son, and he was all right.

Carlton's foster mother led us on a tour of his new home, a home filled with love. We met her son. He couldn't talk and was in his wheelchair unable to propel himself. In silence he seemed to be welcoming us into his home.

She showed us her "bird baby", a child so fragile that he looked as though he might break if you picked him up. His arms and legs were as thin as pencils. He had weighed only ounces at birth and never did fully develop. She had taken bird boy in because others had said he could not live. When she picked him up, his body sank into her loving arms, relaxed and at peace. She said love was keeping him alive and as long as he was with her, he'd receive plenty of it.

She had rubella babies, Downes Syndrome children like Carlton, microcephalics and children with gross deformities in her home. Every person in the home was so severely handicapped that they spent their entire waking moments in their beds. Some seemed ill and others were sitting in their beds with nothing to do. At that time, in the mid sixties, severely handicapped children were treated as if they were sick. Little was done to provide them with activities of any kind. These children were never going to be able to get around on their own.

It was obvious to Mimi and me that Carlton was out of place. This home wasn't prepared for an active child like him. We thanked the woman for being kind to our son and left. We were troubled. We knew that this was just another stopping place for Carlton on his way to God knows where.

On the drive back home a feeling of helplessness permeated the car. Who could we trust? Who should we call? Who will tell us when Carlton is moved again? A move was inevitable. All we wanted to know was where and when, so that we could be a part of it. Again we found prayer to be the only answer for Carlton, We prayed for him and for a decent placement. We prayed for ourselves and for our family. We prayed that we would be able to persevere through these terrible times.

The call came the following Friday. It was from Mr. Pierce. He was happy to inform us that they had finally found our son and had him right there at Pacific State Hospital. He was sorry for any inconvenience he might have caused and assured us that Pacific State Hospital was the finest facility in the state of California. Carlton would be very happy there. He asked us not to visit Carlton for thirty days as Carlton would need a period for adjustment.

Mimi and I were devastated. Carlton's summer trial period at Pacific the previous year had proved to be a disaster. He had come home sick with diarrhea. It took us six months to get him back to any semblance of health. We told Mr. Pierce of our concern and he again assured us things were changing. The state was in the process of placing the severely retarded population into community facilities. He used the term "deinstitutionalization." He assured us that Carlton was high on the list for community placement.

Our hands were tied. Untying them would take a lifetime. We desperately needed a placement for Carlton. We had that placement and it was awful. We had received assurances that meant nothing. We knew in our hearts that if Carlton could only survive Pacific State Hospital, he would be able to move on to other and better places. The old spiritual "Amazing Grace" came to mind. "I once was lost but now I'm found" We had found Carlton but now we were lost. Finding ourselves was going to be a life long process. We placed Carlton in the hands of the Lord.

GLADYS

The spring of 1968 was an exciting time for us. Carlton was holding his own at Bloomington Convalescent Home. Colleen was devouring first grade. She had won a ride on a fire truck with her winning entry in a poster contest. Tommy was in kindergarten with many new friends and Mary Tone as his teacher. Alicia had just turned three and was into everything, and I was awarded a fellowship to study at Syracuse University. The time was perfect for us to leave Crestline and renew old ties to New York State.

By the time we were ready to leave for New York, troubling times had returned. Carlton had been moved from Bloomington Convalescent to Pacific State Hospital and my father had died. We felt we should probably stay put as my mother would need us. She assured us she would be all right so we decided to go to New York and leave Carlton and trust in the Lord to watch over him.

We rented our house in Crestline. We loaded our trailer and van with everything we could take with us for a year at Syracuse. On a sunny August morning we said all of our good-byes and headed toward Pacific State Hospital to say good-bye to Carlton. What we found when we got there was frightening. Carlton, at nine years old, weighed a little more than forty pounds. He had no color and no vitality. We played with him, hugged him, told him we loved him and then took him back to his ward.

Mimi and I were worried about his well being. We were filled with guilt and apprehension, but we had been told that the state was trying to place the children in the State Hospitals into community group homes and Carlton was on the list for placement as soon as possible.

When we got to Syracuse we set up housekeeping in a small two bedroom apartment in student housing. Our contacts with Carlton were sporadic. Friends visited him occasionally and wrote to tell us about their visit and how he was doing. We could read between the lines. We knew he was deteriorating.

One day we received a letter from our social worker saying they had found a group home for Carlton in Fontana as part of the deinstitutionalization program. We were pleased. We knew if Carlton were in a better environment, he'd at least have a chance of making it.

Two weeks later we received a letter from Fontana. In barely legible handwriting, Gladys Belleheumer, Carlton's group home mother, told us how overjoyed she was to have our son. She had chosen him because he looked so in need of love. She was doing everything in her power to nurse him back to health and make him happy in his new home. She told us that if our family or friends wanted to visit him, they were welcome.

Mimi and I were elated. Finally Carlton had found a decent home and the love he needed to survive. We called Gladys. She told us Carlton weighed only thirty eight pounds when he had first come to her He had lost thirty pounds at Pacific State Hospital. She said he was eating well and had already gained eight pounds. We told her that my brother-in-law, Stan, who frequently was in the Fontana area on business, would probably visit her in the near future. Stan did visit and sent us a glowing report with pictures of a very dapper Carlton, dress hat and all.

We heard from Gladys frequently while we were in Syracuse. Often she enclosed a picture of Carlton and his two group home brothers so we could see his improvement. In less than a year in his new home Carlton had gained all his weight back. One time Gladys took the three boys to San Diego to see my mother. My mother, in a letter wrote about the visit with this very loving person who was so good with the boys.

Dear All:

While this letter is written in detail for Mimi and Carl I believe that you will all be happy to hear about the progress Carlton has made. We had a most delightful visit with him and the wonderful Belleheumers. Ray (Mr.) phoned from the zoo at 11 and invited me to meet them but I felt it would be more fun for them to do that part alone and told him I would wait for them here. He said they would make it about three and mentioned the children. I didn't know how many were coming- thot perhaps the son and his family. Tim drove me to the market and as usual I prepared for an army. They did arrive a few minutes after 3 in a large good car; I never know the make, with three boys in seat belts in the back. Mr. and Mrs. G. got out and let Carlton out- he looked so wonderful. Jerry grabbed him and he put his arm around his neck and gave him a big hug as though he really knew him. Then he did the same with me. He laughed and greeted the girls and Tim. Gladys (she insisted I call them Gladys and Ray) is a truly beautiful woman with lovely skin, unlined and so serene. She's heavy but covered her figure with a long muu muu (?) type shift, long beads and so young in appearance. Ray, too, is a fine looking, rugged tho gentle. He's a very remarkable man. I am so filled with admiration for both of them. We went on with Carlton and the rest followed — I thought the other boys about Carlton's size were their grandchildren but they are mongoloids Gladys is now caring for.

My little room gets an overcrowded look with two people in it so Terri took Douglas and Mark outside where she played with them all afternoon. I had a new ball for Carlton. Tim and Brigid played with him — Ray didn't want him to go outside unless they were with him. Those two people simply adore Carlton — he is loving them or they are loving him all the time and their devotion is obvious. They are so proud of every improvement he makes and the most blessed thing for Carlton they firmly believe he will talk and learn. First, physically he is a new child — he is taller and his body is beautiful — the skinny legs are firm and strong and there isn't an ounce of fat on him. I couldn't possibly lift him now and Jerry was amazed when he tried to dance him around as he used to. He is a handsome child and is loved by everyone. Their caseworker comes once a month, a young married man, who is very fond of Carlton. He is working now to get him into school and is sure he's going to make it. I might doubt that but neither G. nor Ray will listen to that kind of negative thinking. Of course, G. is praying that you will let her have him next year. She takes fine care of the other boys but she does not love them — she and Ray claim they have never loved a child of their own any more than they do Carlton. They are persistent in their discipline, never shout but are firm and it is surprising the way the boys obey. Carlton seems to know everything they say. G. is so firm in her belief that he will talk when ready that she persists with the words he does say. She fed him yesterday, perhaps because she felt it would be hard for him here, and she made him say "more" when he wanted more. Also he had to say "drink" when he wanted one. He says "love" and puts it into action with a hug. She doesn't give the children sweets - jello and the like, and is a firm believer in vitamin C. Carlton gets a lot of it. I happened to have a full bottle that Betty had sent me so I gave it to G. They must have had a despairing period for three weeks after Carlton was taken from the hospital. He never smiled, couldn't walk and was in awful condition. G. said she never left his side for thee weeks when he started to respond. He never slept _ 5 O'clock in the morning he was still playing in his bed. Finally the doctor told her they would have to give him sedation — 4 times a day. She couldn't go along with that but gives him one tablet at 4:30, prepares him for bed at 7:30 and at 8 he's asleep for the night. Carlton has an enormous appetite but they feel he needs the food. He is tied loosely in bed and G. believes he likes it as it makes him feel secure. Certainly the results are great. His nose still gives him trouble but all of the bad habits are gone. Finally a tooth has come down from the upper part of his mouth and while it's at an angle they say it will straighten out when the other one appears. At 4:30 we all went out and I made coffee for G. and Ray. Jerry had made her one drink but Ray wouldn't have anything. She said the only time she enjoys a drink is after the boys are in bed. She does smoke a lot.

 The dept. would not allow any other children in the home for three months and I guess they wanted longer than that as they felt Carlton needed the attention. He hasn't minded Douglas and Mark. They are wonderful to him — two delightful children that giggle and laugh all the time. If they see Carlton in trouble, they call "Carlie, Carlie/" They speak better and are dear kids. G. said they come from good families. Carlton follows them and laughs with them. Ray has had the garage converted in a sort of playroom and dining area which they all enjoy. He told me he takes Carlton to the market with him and never has any trouble with him. People always stop to talk with them and to sympathize with Carlton. Ray explains that he is the happiest of children and will not have to worry about wars and taxes.

Ray is quiet and does whatever G, asks — gets things from the car, takes the boys to the bathroom, etc.

We decided to have dinner in here as it was getting chilly. I didn't know how I was going to do it- I feel so inadequate now. But G. told Douglas and Mark to sit on the floor with the box you sent the Christmas things in for a table. They ate without the slightest fuss. Both Ray and G. enjoyed my simple meal — I didn't do anything right as the boys could not eat the vegetable plate I prepared — carrot sticks, etc. They could choke. She gives them salad at every meal but cuts everything fine — Carlton loves salad. I had ham and hot German potato salad and Russian rye bread. I made cupcakes for dessert with lighted candles on for the boys. They all blew them out. As I brought them out the boys insisted we sing "Happy birthday" and we all clapped our hands. They had planned on leaving by 5:30 but it was 7 before they got away. I took Carlton for a long walk — he took my hand and didn't try to get off of the walk. G, and R. said they had enjoyed being with us — felt so at home. They are dying to meet you — we showed them all of the snaps we had — Jeanne's good ones were here. I hated to see the boys put into seat belts — I have such a horror of restraint, but G. said she wouldn't go around the block without them.

When my year in Syracuse drew to a close, I decided not to return to Crestline. Instead I applied for a teaching position in the San Diego area. I told Gladys that we'd be returning in August and we wanted to take Carlton for a family visit. We were thinking about a weekend but Gladys was thinking a week. She sounded tired. She had six retarded children living with her by this time and said she could use the break. She said she would have Carlton ready the day we arrived.

We left Syracuse with the van and trailer packed with a years' accumulation of things, including a newly acquired grandfather's clock and a library table. We planned to meander back to California; sight seeing and stopping here and there for about ten days would be a perfect end to our year of study.

Five days later we were in San Diego. Sightseeing proved a disaster with nowhere to park and the places we planned to visit packed with thousands of families with similar ideas. The trailer had to be unloaded each night so we could sleep in it. It was chaos. We headed west as fast as possible and pulled up to my mother's house on the morning of the fifth day of our trip. I knew she was surprised, though happy, to see us so soon.

That afternoon I found a trailer park fairly close to Mission Bay. We dumped all our stuff at my mother's house and headed to our temporary home by the bay. Once there, we hooked up our fourteen footer and settled down for a week of rest and recreation. The next week I would have to find a permanent place to live and a job. It would not be a good week to bring Carlton to stay with us, but I had promised Gladys that I would.

So the first day of our vacation was a trip to Fontana, one hundred and twenty miles north of San Diego. We would be picking up Carlton so that he too could enjoy family life and vacation with us for a week. The three hour trip was a happy one. We talked about Carlton, about the times when he got into the oysters and the cherries, and the times we couldn't find him. Before we knew it, we pulled up in front of Carlton's new home.

A short, plump woman with dark brown hair and sparkling brown eyes, the image of Mrs. Santa Claus, greeted us holding Carlton in her arms. . He looked nothing like the boy we had seen at Pacific State one year ago. He was smiling and seemed to recognize us. Colleen, Tommy and Alicia stared at their brother. They were still confused about Carlton and why he wasn't at home. Gladys welcomed us. Her face radiated love as she introduced us to her husband Ray and her boys.

Including Carlton, Gladys had six retarded boys in her home. Two boys shared each room. They each had an area for their own special toys, pictures and clothes. Looking at the cards and nick knacks in the rooms, we could tell that Gladys smothered her boys with tender loving care. Her daughter helped her out when she could but most of the time, seven days a week; Gladys did what had to be done. There were no schools for her boys so she had them at home for twenty four hours a day.

Over lunch Gladys brought us up to date on Carlton. She told us how little and frail he was when she first saw him. She had hand fed him for the first few weeks. Carlton had responded to her loving care, putting on weight and becoming quite a personality. Gladys told us she and her husband had remodeled their house to accommodate the boys. Ray kept everything in working order. He fixed whatever needed fixing and built whatever needed building. The work of caring for the boys was hard she admitted, but she wouldn't change places with anyone.

We told her about Carlton and our family, his life while we were living in Crestline, about our year in Syracuse and our plans in San Diego. When she heard we were going to vacation for a week in a trailer park, she laughed and said, "That should be quite an adventure." She assured us that we could bring Carlton back at anytime if things didn't work out. Mimi and I asked her "What could possibly go wrong"? As she watched Colleen, Tommy and Alicia running around, she said "Just in case, you can bring him back whenever you want. I'll miss him".

We left for San Diego where we would have a week of leisure around the pool and at the beach with our whole family. Life couldn't get much better than that. We were young, naive and determined to fool ourselves into believing that Carlton wasn't much of a problem.

It was warm when we arrived at the trailer park that evening so we all went for a swim in the pool. Then we went back to the trailer to get ready for bed. The trailer was small. We had trouble all fitting inside at the same time. We took the table out. We made the dining area into a bed for Carlton and Alicia. Colleen and Tom would sleep on a canvas bunk that pulled out above the double bed where Mimi and I would sleep. If everything worked as planned and everyone was cooperative and everyone was tired, we could all sleep in the trailer. We put our porta potty outside the door just in case, tucked everyone in, turned out the lights and hoped for the best.

Carlton didn't like his new surroundings at all He kept getting out and wandering around the trailer. We put Colleen and Tom in the van and put Carlton in the canvas bed above us. He kept climbing out and falling on Mimi and me. We put Alicia on the canvas bed, Mimi in the dining area and Carlton in bed with me. I was on the outside blocking any escape. He thought we were playing some kind of prison game. He never did go to sleep.

Morning finally came. Breakfast was cold cereal and milk. Mimi and I dressed the kids, then I took them exploring while Mimi made lunches. We planned to go to the bay and then go visit my mother. My mother loved all the kids but had a special place in her heart for Carlton. When we were at her house, she played with Carlton and we had breathing space to relax and enjoy San Diego. Each evening we spent our time at the pool or we went to the local ice cream parlor for a treat. Each night we struggled with our sleeping routine. Mimi and I took turns playing prisoner with Carlton.

When I had to go on job interviews, I dropped Mimi and the children off at my mother's place. No one person in the world could have managed those four kids alone. After two interviews I took a teaching position with the San Diego Unified School District.

My new job called for a celebration dinner at McDonald's. After a scrumptious meal we went for a relaxing evening around the pool. The kids wanted to show me all their new water tricks. Tom and Colleen could dive and swim the length of the pool underwater. Alicia could jump off the side twist in the air and grab the gutter catching herself before she got her hair wet. Carlton could sit on the steps of the pool and make bubbles. I was a very proud father.

Mimi was back at the trailer getting things organized when Alicia showed me her trick for the umpteenth time. This time it didn't quite work. She caught the gutter with her hands alright but she also caught the edge of the pool with her chin. Blood poured out. I grabbed her, covered the cut with a towel and told Colleen to hurry and get Mimi. I needed help getting Carlton and the rest of the clan back to the trailer.

The manager of the park gave us directions to an emergency room. The doctor there put seven stitches into our daughter's chin and told her no swimming for a week. The only recreation we had was the pool and now Alicia couldn't use it.

After another sleepless night, we opted for a day at the San Diego Zoo. The kids had been cooped up for the past nine days. Just being able to run around made the trip worthwhile. Seeing all the animals was icing on the cake. We rented a stroller for Carlton. The kids took turns pushing him, often missing fellow zoo goers by inches, and sometimes not missing at all. After a full day of animals, cotton candy, seal shows and fun we returned to our trailer park home. The next day we would look for a house.

We went house hunting as a family. Landlords said "No" as soon as they saw us coming. Eventually we found an older house near the center of town. The owner said we could move in on Friday. It wouldn't take us long to move in since all we had was a grandfather clock and a library table. Everything else was still in Crestline, a hundred and thirty miles away.

We put the grandfather clock in the living room, the library table in the den and the mattresses from the trailer in the upstairs bedrooms. We put our clothes away. We made a list of what we needed and decided "everything" about covered it. Our new home didn't even have a stove.

The week was up. It was time to return Carlton to Gladys. When we arrived at Gladys's house, Carlton seemed glad to be back with his friends. Gladys looked rested. We told her about our week in the trailer. Alicia showed Gladys her chin. We said we hoped to have Carlton home for visits once or twice a month. We hugged Carlton, said our goodbyes and drove off to our new life in San Diego.

HILLDALE

Hilldale Rehabilitation Center

One afternoon in April 1972, we received a call from Gladys. She was crying as she told us that she had to give up the boys. Because the boys, whom she so loved, consumed so much of their lives her husband, Ray, could take it no more and left. With her husband gone and no one to help, there was no way she could care for six severely handicapped boys. She was a prisoner in her own home. Her health was failing and she was emotionally drained. Her boys had returned to Pacific State Hospital. We assured Gladys that she would always be part of our family, and prepared for another move for Carlton.

A short time later, we received a letter from the Regional Center informing us that Carlton would soon be placed in Hilldale Convalescent Center in La Mesa, only five minutes from our house. We were pleased even though we weren't part of this new placement process, because at last Carlton would be near us. We would be able to help him adjust to his new living situation. We could see him whenever we wanted and play a larger role in his life.

We drove to Hilldale the next day to see his new home. At first glance we mistook it for a motel. On closer inspection we saw it was indeed a large nursing facility. We were warmly welcomed by the facility's administrator, Mrs. Mumford, although she was surprised to see us. She hadn't been made aware that Carlton was coming to Hilldale.

We asked her if we might tour the facility. She was hesitant as we were the first parents of a retarded client to visit the facility. She told us they were in the process of changing Hilldale from a geriatric facility to a facility for the retarded. We entered the main part of the building and were buzzed through large locked double doors and found ourselves in a long hallway. It reminded me of a hospital ward. At a nursing station in the middle of the hallway nurses were doing paperwork. Just past the nursing station, hallways led to many rooms, some with two beds, and some with three. Each room looked exactly the same, walls painted white, no decorations, portable closets attached to a three drawer dresser and a light on the wall behind each bed. Between rooms was a shared bathroom.

A few rooms were occupied, some by retarded people and some by geriatric patients. Mrs. Mumford explained the mixed occupancy and empty rooms were due to the transition from geriatric care to housing retarded patients. She was very excited about the change. She told Mimi and me that the staff was already learning how to deal with retarded patients.

Looking at the geriatric clients still living there and the retarded people who had recently arrived, it was obvious to us that there was little difference in the type of care they were getting. They were all confined to their beds. They were all being treated as though they were sick.

When I asked what the difference in treatment was, she said there was none. They had never dealt with "the retarded" before.

Mimi and I left shaking our heads in amazement. It was hard to imagine what Carlton was going to do at Hilldale. They were prepared for a slow and sick child. Carlton was active and in constant motion. I could picture the staff looking for him morning, noon and night. He was going to need their full attention. If I wasn't mistaken, he was going to be a real pain in the neck for this unsuspecting group.

Carlton arrived early in May of 1972. Mrs. Mumford called and she seemed beside herself with joy. We also got a call from our social worker inviting us to come over to Hilldale to see Carlton's new room and to go over the records that arrived with our thirteen year old son. We were nervous when we got there. We noticed that the geriatric population was gone and the retarded population was growing. The staff seemed to be shell shocked and completely confused by their new clients who were supposed to be passive but were anything but.

Carlton's records were almost nonexistent. His date of birth was incorrect. There was no medical history at all. We remembered filling out volumes when he was first placed at Bloomington and wondered where they might be. We filled in as much as we could remember, and finally got to visit Carlton in his new room. He seemed to be as happy to see us as we were to see him. After a grand reunion we saw that the room hadn't changed since our first visit. It still looked like a hospital room. Carlton seemed no worse for wear, and seeing Mimi and I he was his old happy self. After some more moral boosting hugs we proceeded to see what he had in the way of clothes and toys.

Carlton had left Gladys's home with all his clothes and personal belongings. He had spent about three weeks at Pacific State Hospital before coming to Hilldale. Most of his clothes and personal belongings that had gone with him to Pacific State ended their trip there. We took inventory and made plans to shop with him when he came home the following weekend. Our social worker told us he could only go home during the day for the first month. We decided to get him a new wardrobe on the following Saturday.

We were angry at how the State of California was treating its handicapped people and those who cared for them. They lost Gladys because she couldn't get any free time for herself. Now they were placing their retarded citizens in facilities where the staff was completely untrained. The State called it "deinstitutionalization". I called it institutional transfer to save money. Mimi and I knew more about the needs of the retarded than anyone working at Hilldale. What we didn't know was how we could make a very bad situation any better. At first all we could do was to take Carlton home as often as possible.

We took Carlton home at least once each week during that first year at Hilldale. We hated taking him back after a home visit, and he hated going. We were in a constant state of guilt. Colleen, Tommy and Alicia played with Carlton when he was home. They loved him and told their friends about their retarded brother. Many times one or two of our children's playmates would come over to look at Carlton. They had never seen a retarded kid and wanted to see what one looked like. They looked and saw a child just like themselves. They usually stayed to play then left wondering what the big deal was.

During that time the State was removing the retarded from hospitals and placing them, when possible, closer to their homes. It wasn't long before Hilldale filled its fifty seven beds with severely retarded individuals of all ages. Many of the residents were teenagers, some were in their twenties and many were in their thirties and forties. None were toilet trained because it was commonly believed that it wasn't possible to train the severely retarded. None were expected to feed themselves because "the severely retarded couldn't use forks or spoons." They weren't able to dress themselves, wash themselves, comb their hair or chew their food. With these shortcomings, they weren't allowed to go to school. The staff was trying to do everything for the residents. It was an impossible task. These helpless souls were very active. The staff had to catch them first before they could help them.

The workers who had worked with geriatric patients quit as soon as they realized the difficulties involved in working with the retarded population. Every time Mimi and I went to Hilldale, we were greeted by newer and younger faces. Within six months, the staff had changed from middle aged men and women to high school aged boys and girls. The care had degenerated from trying to meet each person's needs to warehousing fifty seven severely disabled persons. Through it all, Mrs. Mumford still cheerfully greeted us, oblivious to the disaster that was taking place down the hall. It was appalling.

By the end of the year, the program for the residents of Hilldale was to awaken them and feed them in the dining room or their room, whichever was easier. After breakfast the residents were strapped to chairs lining the main hallway. This kept them from wandering all over the building. Aides started at one end of the row of chairs and moved down the line changing everyone's diapers. When they got to the end, they worked their way down the other side. When they reached the starting point, they were ready to begin the process again. When they weren't changing the residents they were feeding them. On weekends the schedule was different. On Saturday and Sunday the staff didn't get the residents out of bed. They didn't give them breakfast either.

In order to save money, the staff used only cold water for cleaning so an awful stench permanently permeated the building. We complained, but our complaints fell on deaf ears. Mrs. Mumford countered our complaints by telling us how well things were going. It was unbelievable. Mimi and I knew if anything was to be done, we would have to do it ourselves.

Mimi and I visited other types of programs and living facilities for people like Carlton including The Home of Guiding Hands, a large residential home, under the auspices of the Methodist Church. It was the finest facility of its kind in the state. It consisted of many units, each housing between twelve and twenty-four retarded residents. Each housing unit was designed to provide a homelike setting for the persons living there. The bedrooms displayed personal items belonging to the occupant. Each home had a dining area with small tables and recreation areas with TVs and games. It had playgrounds and a large community swimming pool with a lifeguard in attendance during the day. The Home had many amenities that were specifically designed for the retarded residents. It was the model for community settings for the retarded in the early 1970s.

Home of Guiding Hands had an excellent volunteer program. The volunteers became friends with the residents, playing with them, eating with them, swimming with them and just being there for their friends. The volunteers made it possible for the retarded residents to do things they couldn't do with the staff. Mimi and I thought volunteers might help us make Hilldale a decent place for Carlton and his friends too.

Soon after Carlton was placed at Hilldale, we met a wonderful nun, Sister Maxine Kraemer who ran Saint Madeline Sophies, a school for the retarded.

Sister Kraemer

One day I mentioned Carlton to her and told her that he wasn't able to go to any school. Sr. Kraemer performed a bonified miracle. I'll testify to it if she ever comes up for sainthood. She pleaded Carlton's case to the various agencies that placed children in her school and within a week Carlton was enrolled in Saint Madeline Sophies. School got Carlton out of his hallway chair and away from Hilldale every day. It also introduced Mimi and me to a group of dedicated people, who, over the years, would help us bring Hilldale into the twentieth century.

When Carlton arrived at school each day, the teachers and aides at Saint Madeline Sophies could tell by his appearance that things weren't good at Hilldale. His hair wasn't combed, his clothes weren't clean and often they could identify what he'd had for breakfast by looking at his face. His lunches were inadequate. Hilldale never sent a change of clothes for him so they were always scrambling to find him something for him to wear when he needed a change. When they asked the people at Hilldale to wash Carlton's face every day and send a clean set of clothes, their pleas fell on deaf ears. When there was no response from Hilldale, they asked Mimi and me to work with Hilldale on improving the situation.

At first, our efforts on Carlton's behalf were not well received. When the administration and staff at Hilldale saw that we were not going to give up, they decided to cooperate, but even then, things didn't improve much. It did open some doors, however. They knew that Mimi and I were interested in Carlton's welfare and that we were going to monitor everything they did. They knew we were disappointed in the facility, and that we wanted to be involved in our son's life. Slowly but surely Mrs. Mumford began to talk to us about some of the problems she was having.

In one of our conversations, I suggested that I might be able to bring in volunteers on Saturday mornings. We could start some activity programs for the residents. Mrs. Mumford gave me the go ahead and so began a Saturday morning volunteer program. Hilldale would never be the same.

Enjoying time with Carlton at Hilldale. Form left Tom, Garrett (Tom's son), me and Carlton. Carlton is in his 30's in this picture

MRS. MUMFORD

Carlton and I at Hilldale in the 1980's. Carlton is in his 30's in the picture. Behind us are the lockers that held residents' clothing and personal care items

Mrs. Mumford, the administrator of Hilldale Convalescent Center had been the secretary at Hilldale when it was a geriatric facility. She became the administrator when it became a residential care facility for the retarded.

Mrs. Mumford tried to please everyone. She had a heart of gold. She loved the retarded residents living at Hilldale. She loved their parents but felt sorry for them. She loved her staff and tried to be their mother confessor. She loved her company and her superiors and wanted them to think highly of her. She could change a subject before it was ever discussed. She was one of those people who could hurt you with their love.

Through most of the twenty years that I knew her, I can only describe our relationship as strained. She was the administrator of Hilldale and I am a parent of a child living at Hilldale. Our backgrounds were very different. I have a master's degree in Special Education. I was a member of the state board for the Developmentally Disabled. I was teaching courses on retardation at the local community college and I knew what was being done to make quality care for retarded persons a reality.

She had been secretary of a geriatric facility and was now in charge of a facility for retarded people, a group she knew nothing about. She wanted the parents to be happy with Hilldale so she shielded them from everything that they might not like to hear. She only shared the good things that happened at Hilldale, never anything bad. After Carlton was at Hilldale for about a year, Mimi and I realized that the only person we had any contact with at Hilldale was Mrs. Mumford. If we saw another parent, an aide or a nurse, "Hello" was about as far as any conversation went. Actually the nurses and aides usually disappeared when we they saw us coming. They had been instructed not to talk to us. It might cause us to worry.

When I had a question or a complaint, Mrs. Mumford would say," Oh Mr. Smith, I'll see that that's taken care of right away. "Don't you worry." She said the same thing for the eighteen years that she was at Hilldale, although we told her many times that we were very concerned about Carlton's well-being.

Mrs. Mumford must have put in an eighty hour week. If I went in to Hilldale at eleven at night, she would be trying to cut the cost of termite control. If I went in the morning, she'd be mopping the floor. At noon I'd find her eating her lunch at her desk. I think she stayed to make sure nobody on her staff talked to me. If I complained about anything, she handled my complaint by doing something herself that should be done by an aide. One time I told her about a missing jacket that belonged to Carlton. She sorted the laundry of the fifty seven residents for over two hours looking for it. Finally, I didn't complain about anything because I didn't want to take her away from her work.

In time I learned to work around Mrs. Mumford. Whenever I saw other parents at Hilldale, I went out of my way to talk to them. The more we talked, the more we found we had in common. I learned we all had the same problem, Mrs. Mumford.

I taught a course at Grossmont College on mental retardation. I suggested to the people working at Hilldale that it might be a good for them to take my course. Many of them did and learned through my course that I was trustworthy. They began filling me in on what was going on at Hilldale.

In time I was able to confront Mrs. Mumford with anonymous parent complaints. I could also bring up the areas I had discovered through my students that needed improvement

The more I found out about Hilldale's shortcomings, the more paranoid Mrs. Mumford became. However, even with my knowing what was going on, she still tried to give me the impression that all was well. If I knew something was unsanitary, she'd deny it or say it was all taken care of. Then after I left she'd take care of it. At least I knew my complaints were being heard, even if they weren't being taken care of in a permanent way. This went on for almost two years, then, with the help of our Social Worker, we decided to bring the parents together as a group.

The social worker who was assigned to us by Regional Center, Nancy Seppella, was the one ray of light at Hilldale. She had the same communication problem with Mrs. Mumford that I had. Nancy's job was to see that Hilldale met all the requirements of the state. If she saw something that wasn't right, she told the nurse, an aide or Mrs. Mumford about it so it could be made right. If Hilldale didn't correct it, the Regional Center with Licensing could take away Hilldale's license to operate. If Hilldale and Regional Center worked together, the improvements would make Hilldale a better place. It never worked because Mrs. Mumford considered Nancy the enemy. Every time Nancy came into Hilldale the staff went the other way. Every time Nancy made a suggestion, it was considered an insult. Nancy realized the parents of residents living at Hilldale were being kept away from one another. She called me one day and asked if I would be willing to form a parents group with her help. By this time I'd have done anything to see things improve.

We decided that I would suggest the idea of a parent's group for Hilldale to Mrs. Mumford, telling her I would be willing to get it started. I explained how a parents group could help Hilldale with money other things Hilldale needed. I asked her to think about it. It wasn't too long before she told Nancy about a great idea she had, forming a parents group for Hilldale. Nancy agreed it was great idea and so the Families and Friends of Hilldale was born.

Nancy and I wrote a letter to all the parents inviting them to a first meeting at Nancy's office. Over twenty five parents showed up. Most of them were extremely angry with the way things were going. We spent most of the night complaining about food, clothes, cleanliness, nursing, communication, air conditioning, activities, access and Mrs. Mumford. After everyone had had their say, we decided to meet once a month to support each other and improve Hilldale.

I became spokesman for the group. With twenty five parents behind me, I could say to Mrs. Mumford, "One of the parents told me--- ". At the next meeting I reported her responses back to the parents. Every once in awhile Mrs. Mumford came to one of our meetings. When she came, no one complained. We just sat there and listened to far out excuses for whatever had been criticized. She honestly thought that because the parents wanted Hilldale to be a nice place for their sons and daughters, it satisfied them just to hear everything was fine.

The parents group organized itself into a non-profit organization so we could raise money for Hilldale, a for-profit facility. That way we could get donations and purchase equipment for the residents. We didn't raise a lot of money because we had no way to raise it. Every once in a while someone gave us a hundred dollars or we had a yard sale and raised a few dollars. There were no major donations those first few years.

Hilldale desperately needed a wheel-chair equipped van to transport the residents to various activities. The parents felt the owner should provide one, but he never offered and Mrs. Mumford never asked him. The parents group decided to get Hilldale a van by collecting Betty Crocker coupons. Mrs. Mumford thought that was a marvelous idea. She would even get her church to help. We had our friends, our churches and anyone else we could think of save their coupons for us. Each meeting we tallied the coupons up and resolved to go out and collect some more.

One month we invited the owner, Mr. Bauer, and Mrs. Mumford to our meeting so we could update them on our project. We told them how much we appreciated what they were doing for our children. We gave them the good news that we had, in just five months, collected fifteen thousand Betty Crocker coupons. We also gave them the not so good news that we still needed a little over three million more coupons. We hoped to have the remainder of the coupons within the next ten years. Two weeks later Mr. Bauer purchased a van for Hilldale. Betty Crocker gave us two hundred dollars for our coupons. Our initial effort had proven to be an overwhelming success.

Our parent group always asked Mrs. Mumford what we could purchase that would really be useful for the residents. We were thinking playground equipment, TVs or something along that line. Her suggestion was a case of shoelaces, white. She said they were always looking for shoelaces. She could keep them in her office so she'd know where they were. That Christmas our major gift for Hilldale was a case of white shoelaces.

The next Christmas, with serious reservations, I asked her what that year's gift should be. After a great deal of soul searching she decided our major gift should be a hundred pair of white sox. That way the residents would always have sox that matched even if some were lost. Who could argue with that?

Mrs. Mumford was always distrustful of her staff and for good reason. She suspected they were robbing Hilldale blind and they were. I always believed that the staff felt whatever they took was a fringe benefit for hard work and little pay. After three months of faithful service a new staff member was guaranteed a three cent an hour raise. It was no wonder things were always missing.

I lost a good jacket at one of our meetings. One time five indoor plants disappeared. But the real scandal was the discovery that over thirty florescent light bulbs were missing. Mrs. Mumford called special staff meetings, appealed to them, shamed them, bribed them, anything to get the pilfering to cease. She knew the aides were taking clothes, bedding and even some of the resident's candy, but she could never find out who was doing it. She fired the ones she was suspicious of, but still the stealing went on. It was as though it were a game to drive Mrs. Mumford crazy. One year all the Christmas gifts and the cookies for the Christmas party vanished. Anything the parents group gave to Hilldale during that time was bolted to the wall or floor for safe keeping.

The bedding at Hilldale deteriorated rapidly. The sheets and blankets in most cases had to be washed daily. They were washed in a commercial washing machine so they really took a beating and were useless within a few months. We told Mrs. Mumford that we felt the blankets on the beds were unacceptable. We wanted new blankets to be purchased. The parents group even offered to pay for half the cost of new blankets. She as usual defended the tattered blankets, saying they were wonderful and everything was just fine.

A few days later she took us up on our offer and ordered all new blankets for the residents' beds. We were pleased, but time went by and we saw no new blankets. After about two months the parents inquired about the blankets at one of our meetings. Mrs. Mumford who was at the meeting burst with happiness when the subject came up. The blankets had arrived and were in her office. In fact they had been there for several weeks. It would be her pleasure to show them to us. She led us into her office and opened up a locked cabinet full of new blankets for all of us to see. The blankets were beautiful, but we asked if it might be better to display them on the beds. With her voice becoming high pitched and her speech accelerating, she sputtered. "Well I would have liked that too, but because of all the thefts that were taking place, I felt I couldn't put them out all out at once or they were sure to be stolen, so in order to keep that from happening she was letting only one go out at a time. We offered to buy her a surveillance system for the facility the following Christmas, so she could monitor the blankets from her office.

Mrs. Mumford was underpaid. She worked hard to save her company money. She loved the residents. She was concerned for the young people on her staff and frequently loaned them money. She picked them up when they had no way to get to work. Often she had special treats for them. She served the residents breakfast when she was short of help. She did the laundry if the laundry people didn't make it to work. She was one of those dedicated people who were in a position that was way over her head.

We parents were never comfortable with Mrs. Mumford but we grew to love her. Through all the years that she administered Hilldale she never burdened us with anything she thought we couldn't handle. Whatever she did, she did it out of goodness not malice. When our sons and daughters were sick she didn't tell us for fear we would worry. If one of the residents had an accident or died, we'd hear about it from someone other than Mrs. Mumford. She never wanted us to be upset.

She even grew to trust our family enough that Alicia worked at Hilldale for two years toward the end of Mrs. Mumford's career. Alicia has a natural curiosity and would have been a great private eye. She never misses thing but through the years Alicia worked at Hilldale there was nothing major to report…and trust me, she looked. I hope that Mrs. Mumford realized that by the end of her tenure at Hilldale there was really not that much to be upset about.

Carlton at Hilldale with a few of the workers in the 1980's. Alicia is on Carlton's left she was working at Hilldale at the time. Notice how young the workers are and the lack of any scrubs. Very different than today!

When she retired the parents wanted to do something special for her. We talked and talked about it and decided to give her a gift certificate to the Bible Book Store as she was a religious person. She took the gift certificate and bought Bibles for a missionary in a poor area of Mexico. That's the kind of person she was.

At her retirement party I presented her with this letter:

November 8, 1989
Dear Mrs. Mumford,

The Families and Friends of Hilldale would like to sincerely thank you for all the hard work and loving care you have given to our sons and daughters. For our children, Hilldale has been a second home. Through your loving concern for each one of them, you have helped us appreciate how dedication can enhance someone's life.

You have guided Hilldale from the dark ages to where we are today. Through all these years and all the changes, your love and leadership has been a shining beacon. Your long hours have been an inspiration. Many times your notes of encouragement and understanding have helped us, as parents, keep the faith.

It would be wonderful if our sons and daughters could thank you personally for all you have done but sadly, through no fault of their own, most are unable to express their love to you. We hope you realize the impact you have had on their lives and how much it has been appreciated.

Silent prayers are being offered for you daily...prayers for a long life... prayers for happiness...prayers for joy with your family...prayers of friendship...and prayers of peace. I'm sure the Lord has a special place for anyone who reaches out to retarded children and you certainly are entitled to reap the rewards that come from a life dedicated to helping these special people.

Please enjoy your retirement. You will be missed. You are truly loved.

Love and Friendship,
The Families and Friends of Hilldale
Carl F. Smith, President

ANOTHER CHRISTMAS STORY

Carlton taking in the Christmas when he was about 7 years old

Christmas at Hilldale was never a time of celebration. The season came and went almost unnoticed until the year Bob Martin put on the Christmas Pageant.

When I first met Bob, he was a volunteer. To Bob the residents weren't severely retarded persons. They were just another group of folks who needed a little light in their life.

Nothing was impossible to Bob. He initiated our field trips. If there was a place to go or something to see, he felt everyone at Hilldale should go and see it. Sometimes it took us longer to get ready, load buses and get there than it took to witness the event. That didn't matter to Bob. The important thing was for the residents to be part of the excitement.

It wasn't long before Bob became program director at Hilldale. Bob organized volunteers to take residents to movies, parties and special events that were taking place throughout the city. He even started a Boy Scout troop complete with campouts.

Bus trips and special events weren't enough for Bob. He decided the residents would put on a Christmas Pageant, the story of the birth of Christ. When he first told me of his plan in September, I thought he had really lost it. I'd been involved with so many school Christmas shows that I knew a Christmas Pageant with severely retarded actors was ridiculous, especially at Hilldale. The only room large enough for a performance was the dining room that was used to feed the residents three times a day. It didn't seem to bother Bob that there was no place to practice or perform the show and that the actors and actresses were severely retarded.

Soon after Bob told me about his project, he went to work assigning roles, getting costumes, making sets that were very portable and writing a non verbal script. Mary, Joseph, the Christ Child, the three kings and the innkeeper would be the main characters in the pageant. The rest of the residents would be shepherds and angels.

Shepherds and angels were easy. Anyone who was confined to a wheel chair was an angel. Properly costumed they would appear to be floating around the stage, their wheel chairs camouflaged as clouds. Shepherds were the residents who were ambulatory but unable to stand still for any length of time. The main characters came from the higher functioning persons who could, with help, follow simple directions. Though the parts called for little stage direction and few words, the main actors spent weeks rehearsing their roles.

Bob's choice of actors and actresses for the leading roles in the pageant echoed the true meaning of Christmas. The Christ Child was Marcus, a black child born without arms or legs who always had a sparkle in his peaceful, understanding eyes. He was the essence of the Christ Child, a perfect choice for the central role.

Mary and Joseph were chosen for their ability to kneel and say a few words. Bob chose Faye, the oldest person living at Hilldale, to be Mary. Faye was the perfect Mary; she welcomed everyone who came into the facility. She had no family of her own. As Mary, Faye finally had the family she always wanted.

John cast as Joseph, could talk and learn a few lines. He would be able to tell Mary how beautiful their child was. With many rehearsals he could also ask the innkeeper if there was any room at the inn.

Arnie was the innkeeper. All Arnie ever said at Hilldale was "No!" Bob figured Arnie already had his part memorized. It was only natural to cast him in that roll.

Bob rehearsed every afternoon between lunch and dinner. Rehearsals were difficult because they took place on an imaginary stage. The actors had no concept of the finished product and repeating the same thing over and over again had no meaning for them. Once Bob got the sets together the actors did better.

Bob's sets were simple, a cardboard inn and an outside stable. The main ingredient of the set was hay. Bob had six bales of hay delivered to Hilldale two weeks before the performance. He planned to spread the hay from one bale all over the stage area, and place the other five bales around the performing area for the entrances and exits of shepherds and angels.

The loose hay part of the set had to wait for opening night since the dining room had to be ready for dinner each night. However, at each rehearsal the bales were placed as they would be for the performance so the actors could get a feel for their entrances and exits. After rehearsal Bob stacked the bales of hay in a corner of the dining room so dinner could be served.

On the night of the performance every available chair was needed for the audience. Setting up the dining room for the pageant took so long that dinner had to be served throughout the facility instead of in the dining room. After dinner all fifty seven residents had to be costumed and ready to perform. The performance was to begin at seven thirty, which gave the staff and volunteers two and a half hours to feed, clean, and costume the fifty seven performers, set up the theater and welcome guests to Hilldale.

Word of the Christmas Pageant had spread to parents, families and friends. Bob was surprised on the night of the performance to find Hilldale jammed with first nighters eagerly awaiting the Christmas Story. People kept coming and coming until every seat was taken. Still they came, standing in the aisles and finally crowded into the patio looking in through the doors where the three kings were to make their entrance. The dining room was so crowded the stage had to be halved to accommodate the overflow, making it difficult for the angels and shepherds who were waiting behind the haystacks.

At seven thirty the dining room lights dimmed and the stage lights came up. One of the hidden shepherds who was allergic to straw, sneezed. In the center of the stage, covered with hay, was a manger. Placed strategically, bales of hay gave the scene the appearance of a stable. Off to stage left, a cardboard refrigerator box bore a sign saying "Inn". Mary and Joseph entered looking very holy. Every now and then they looked toward the audience and waved. They couldn't see anything because of the bright lights but they knew we were there.

Bob was narrator. As he read, Faye and John were to go to the inn, knock on the door and ask Arnie if there was any room for them to have a baby. John knocked a little too hard, the inn fell on top of Arnie and Arnie immediately said "No!" John then asked Arnie if there was room at the inn. Arnie said "No!" Joseph and Mary just stood there. Arnie said "No!" The audience heard Bob say "Arnie close the door!" Arnie said "No!" We could see Arnie being pulled away from the door so the play could go on. We continued to hear Arnie repeating his only line.

Bob went on with the narration. The scene shifted to the stable. John led Faye to the manger. He said, "Faye you feel okay?" Faye mumbled "Yes" smiled and waved toward the darkness. An aide came out and placed Marcus in the Manger. He faced the audience and beamed enjoying his moment in the sun. Mary and Joseph knelt looking at their child. They too beamed and waved as the audience applauded this wondrous Christmas scene.

As a volunteer prepared the three kings for their entrance, Bob narrated the story of the heavenly chorus. Shepherds and angels started coming out on the stage from all directions. The wheelchair angels seemed to float on clouds. The shepherds waved and walked around the manger greeting Marcus. Some kept right on walking into the audience looking for hugs. Throughout the audience you could hear parents calling out to their sons and daughters. Mimi and I saw our shepherd son and swelled with pride.

By now the audience was in tears. Through all the commotion the wise men made their entrance. Robed royally Jim, Tony and Marie gracefully approached the Christ Child bearing gifts described by Bob as gold, incense and myrrh. They looked around the audience for their families as they approached the manger. Jim saw his mom and dad and called out, "Hi Mom Hi Dad!" and decided to sit with them. Before he got there one of the volunteers got him rerouted toward the stage. As he got back on track, he called back to his parents, "Bye Mom Bye Dad!"

When the Wise Men arrived at the manger, they all said "Hi!" to John, Faye and Marcus. They put their gifts in the crib and joined the Holy Family the Innkeeper, the shepherds and the angels. Bob told how the heavens resounded in beautiful song when the wise men gave the Child gifts. Then Bob and the audience joined the cast in singing Christmas Carols. The chorus left the stage. Singing and hugging filled the dining room.

The Pageant was over the audience was drained. They had witnessed the impossible. The Christmas Story had never been told more beautifully. The actors were in their glory. The playgoers were jubilant. It was a show worthy of Broadway.

Long after the actors had left the stage and gone to bed, Bob was in the dining room, cleaning up the hay and getting the place ready for breakfast. All the weeks of preparation had culminated in the show of a lifetime. Bob knew there'd never be another show like it. For that one evening Hilldale had become Bethlehem, the residents had become the original cast and the audience had become the shepherds who had been there on opening night.

SCHOOL DAYS

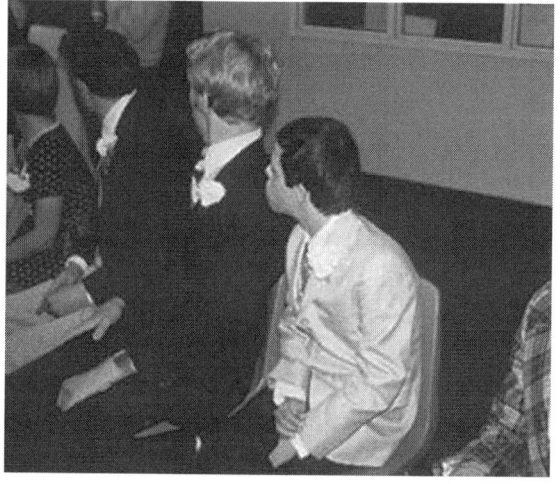

A very attentive Carlton graduating from High School at age 21

Carlton moved to Hilldale in San Diego when Gladys could no longer take care of him. His program at Hilldale consisted of sitting on a chair in the hallway. He had been there almost two years when Mimi and I met Sister Maxine Kraemer. Sister Kraemer was in charge of St. Madeline Sophies, a small school for retarded children. We told her about Carlton. She said she would get him funded and enrolled at St. Madeline Sophies. Mimi and I didn't believe that was possible but she did it.

Carlton was the first child living in a residential care facility to be admitted to her school. By getting Carlton into her program, she opened a door for all retarded children living in institutions such as Hilldale.

Sister Kraemer scraped, begged and borrowed to see that her children received the best program that was humanly possible. The state gave her nine dollars a day per child to run her school. She was a Catholic nun so the bishop supported her with his blessing and nothing more. The school was supported by her Order and the hard work and constant fund raising Sr. Kraemer did to keep it going even as changes were being forced upon her. The rest of the money came from fund raisers and benefactors who were moved by what she was doing.

She had a vision and the determination to see her dream through. Wherever there was a need for a program for the developmentally disabled she saw that it was developed. She started her school because there were no schools for severely retarded children. When public schools were mandated, she lost all her students. She saw a need for an infant program and developed it. Again public schools began infant programs and she lost all her infants. At that time, there were few programs for the developmentally disabled adults so St. Madeline Sophies became an adult training center.

Over the years this program has grown to serve over one hundred twenty five individuals who are learning on the job work skills. Most of the men and women are gainfully employed in jobs that range from maid services, landscaping and food service to employment in the clothing industry. Sister Kraemer was a pioneer and a leader in the struggle for human rights for the Developmentally Disabled.

Carlton was in the basic skills program at St. Madeline Sophies learning to dress and feed himself. These were difficult tasks to learn because of the lack of clothing and poor quality of food that came with him daily from Hilldale.

At St. Madeline Sophies we were able to observe Carlton through one way glass and we were amazed at his progress. He was doing things we never thought he would be able to do. Like many parents who had placed their children in residential programs, we underestimated how much these children could accomplish.

Meanwhile most of the other residents of Hilldale were not involved in any programs even though many were of school age. As president of the Families and Friends of Hilldale I invited experts in to speak to the parents about programs that were available for our sons and daughters. In 1975 I invited the person in charge of the Special Education program at the local school district to speak. He told us that children like ours were excluded because of the severity of their handicap and that minimal requirements of toilet training and speech were necessary for the school to admit them. I asked about the possibility of having a school program at Hilldale. He said he would give it some thought but that's the last we heard about it until about a year later when the same gentleman called and asked if he might speak to the parents again. He wanted to bring us up to date on the new Public Law. At our next meeting he told us that things had changed dramatically since his last visit. Then school was closed to our boys and girls; now he was there to tell us that it was mandated that these same boys and girls go to school. Beginning in September every school aged child living at Hilldale would be in a public school whether we wanted them to go there or not. The parents were bewildered. First there was no way their child could go to school, now he or she had to. Times were changing fast.

Carlton, because of Public Law 94-142, attended Viking Center, a program for severely handicapped high school aged boys and girls in the Grossmont High School District. At age eighteen, for the first time in his life, Carlton was enrolled in a public school program that was fully funded. The teachers were credentialed to work with severely handicapped persons. It wasn't long before many severely handicapped students were found to be far less handicapped than the schools had anticipated. Many moved into programs that were serving the higher functioning.

Carlton remained in his program at Viking and was able to develop personal relationships with some of his classmates. He was toilet trained and learned to sign for food, drink and bathroom. On one occasion Carlton's teacher told us that if Carlton failed to meet one of his goals it was probably her fault because Carlton knew what he was doing and she didn't.

During the years Carlton was at Viking, Mimi and I became aware of the tragedy of all the lost years that Carlton was warehoused and dismissed as being hopeless. Today the parents of children with handicaps receive help from the moment the child is born. These children, their parents and society have benefited greatly by this early intervention. In most cases it has made it possible for the parents to keep their child at home where the care is better and the cost is less.

Even though I was pleased that Carlton was in a public school program, I knew he would be back doing nothing at Hilldale in less than three years. I was putting on workshops for parents to make them aware of what would be in store for their severely handicapped sons and daughters when they turned twenty-one. Progress was being made for infant and school aged children but once these children reached the age of twenty-one, there was nothing. I urged parents to lobby for lifetime programs while their children were still young.

Mimi and I had mixed emotions when Carlton "graduated" from high school. Joy was not one of them. We attended the graduation ceremony to affirm the teachers. They had done a wonderful job. As far as Carlton was concerned, we wondered what he had graduated from and what he had graduated to. We felt a better term would have been "kicked out". He was graduating from an enriched program to no program at all. All the years of encouraging parents to plan ahead had lead to this day. Carlton was going back to Hilldale with no program. Unless a program was found, the progress he had made during the past three years would soon be forgotten. He was sure to be undone. It was sad.

As more handicapped young adults were now "graduating" from school programs the State realized that parents, residential facilities and caretakers couldn't be expected to fill the void left by graduation. Programs other than sheltered workshops had to be found for severely handicapped people over twenty-one. These programs would have to be funded and they would have to be accessible to all persons. Transportation and accountability would have to be a part of the program. Many agencies were brought together to set up a system of adult education that would offer basic skills for some and for others sheltered workshops and meaningful work experiences. Carlton, along with many other graduates of Developmental Centers like Viking, was inappropriate for a sheltered workshop. The agencies decided that adult programs for Severely Handicapped should be placed under the auspices of nonprofit agencies such as Association for Retarded Children, Cerebral Palsy, United Way or programs like St. Madeline Sophies. This began on a small scale with limited funding.

Six months after his "graduation," Carlton had his first experience in a post high school program. He entered a program in rooms rented from a church. Out of curiosity Mimi and I visited the program. We found Carlton seated at a large picnic table in a small room. There were no classroom materials, books magazines or toys. There were no decorations on the walls. There were no bulletin boards. The teacher had her eight students sitting at the table doing paper work. They each had a crayon and a mimeographed picture. They were supposed to color the picture. We asked her what she was hoping to accomplish and she said she was trying to keep her eight students occupied at the table by having them color or sort objects that she had collected herself. She was a nice person, dedicated to her charges, ill prepared and poorly paid for her assignment.

While we were there four of the students quit coloring and reclined on the floor. Two had their heads down asleep at the table. One was scribbling away and Carlton was eating his crayon. We asked her how things were working out. She shook her head and said, "Not too good". Adult programs left much to be desired. There were no trained teachers or teachers' aides. There were no programs, no facilities and no direction, but at least they had begun.

After Carlton had been in the program for about two weeks we were called to a meeting by the program director and his staff to discuss his progress. Mimi went to the meeting armed with a tape recorder so that I might be able to hear what was discussed. Before the meeting began Mimi asked the director if she might tape the meeting. He said it would be fine. The program director began by telling Mimi problem after problem that Carlton had. After he had finished elaborating on every problem possible, there was silence. Finally the silence was broken by Mimi's quiet voice. Controlling her anger, she said "Maybe Carlton doesn't have these problems, maybe you and your staff have the problem of finding the key to Carlton." Again there was silence. When the director regained his composure he closed the meeting by saying the school was unable to meet Carlton's needs so he was terminated. Fortunately, he meant Carlton's stay in the program was terminated, not Carlton.

Back at Hilldale Carlton returned to his program of eating, sleeping and free time. Our social worker kept looking for programs that would accommodate our son. She eventually found Unyeway, a nonprofit agency set up to offer day programs for the Severely Handicapped on an Indian

Reservation about a forty five minute bus ride from Hilldale. The classrooms were set up in a large hall. While there, Carlton did the usual sorting, organizing and coloring. He also took walks and worked in the garden. The teachers and aides were learning by doing. They were ill prepared and poorly paid, but like everyone we've ever met through these programs, they were dedicated to their students Carlton was doing well on the Reservation until Unyeway was forced to move because the hall was needed for a Casino.

A remodeled old store in El Cajon became the new home for the Unyeway program for the disabled. After that the program moved to an industrial park in Lakeside. Through the moves, Carlton remained at Unyeway. His program was refined throughout the years to can crushing, paper sorting and discriminating shopping. Discriminating shopping meant going to the Seven Eleven store to choose his own candy bar. Crushing cans and sorting newspapers helped raise money to purchase materials for the classrooms. The teachers and aides are dedicated to and optimistic for their students. Most accept wages below poverty level. Already under funded, when budget cuts are made in the state the severely handicapped are first on the list for less money. It is easy to slash funds for people that don't vote.

Soon after the Razavis' family over the ownership of Hilldale, it became apparent to them that the adult programs left much to be desired. Hilldale depended on Regional Center to furnish programs and transportation for their residents. The residents were placed in many programs all starting at different times. Mornings were chaotic at Hilldale as some buses arrived as early as 6:30.

Out of frustration, Mr. Razavi, (Daruish) decided to purchase vans to transport the residents. This helped by making the mornings more manageable, but it wasn't enough for Daruish. He didn't care for the adult programs his residents were attending so he began an adult program of his own. He rented some storefronts in a mall not too far from Hilldale and he staffed it carefully. The name of the new program would be the Advantage Center.

At our request Carlton was moved from Unyeway to the Advantage Center program where he thrived. The staff had a Variety of programs from basic skills, arts and crafts, and community awareness to a modified sheltered workshop. Advantage Center was Carlton's last adult program. He did well there. It became obvious what a good program could do for the Carltons of the world.

What did school mean to Carlton? It's hard to say. Some say it's a waste of time and money. Others feel it keeps this particular group of individuals busy. Mimi and I and others involved with these programs have found them to be invaluable. Adult programs were a key part of Carlton's life as they are for all severely handicapped persons. They have opened new horizons. They gave Carlton a friend. They gave others self esteem by enabling them to work like the rest of us. They give those who work in the programs the satisfaction of helping others attain some semblance of normalcy in their lives. Is it worth it? It is if you can place a value on every person no matter what their gifts.

AGE APPROPRIATE

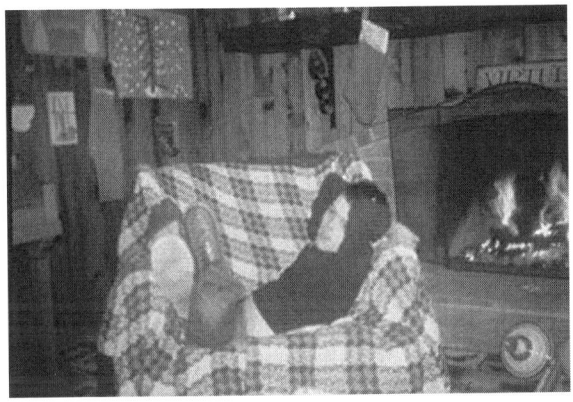

Carlton watching football on New Year's Day. He loved any kind of a ball. In this picture Carlton is in his late 20's

When Carlton approached his thirty fourth birthday, I found myself again at odds with the "system". Still, it was a system made up of people who truly wanted the best for the developmentally disabled, but were unable to communicate with one another, the system caused as much confusion as it caused good.

Apparently the main job of parents of severely handicapped offspring, especially children who have reached adulthood was to sign documents. These same parents were usually the last to be consulted on issues pertaining to their own child. The documents that they signed were the IPP's, (Individual Program Plan) IEP's, (Individual Education Plan) medical forms, school forms and any other forms that confirmed they're being part of the process. Signing forms was supposed to bring normalcy to our children. If for any reason a parent failed to sign a form, heaven forbid. Surprisingly life went on without the parent's signature. The person the form was about signed his or her mark. The mark is witnessed by someone who then signed the form as witness.

All this signing of forms protected the system and those in the system, so perhaps the forms were useful. In some cases they may even have done some good. These forms, however, were both the basis and the result of much of the legislation that has been put forth by the State of California. If a law is passed, the law must be followed; even if the law might have a detrimental effect on some of those it is intended to help. All too often, the segment overlooked when rules and laws were put into effect were the severely retarded.

In the early seventies, I attended a meeting of parents and professionals to clarify all the forms that had to be filled out and signed by all sorts of people; parents, doctors, psychologists, social workers, pharmacists, teachers, dentists etc. etc. I was up to my ears in forms. One time after I signed form after form, someone said, "Now give me the keys." I said "Keys to what?" he said "Your car, you just signed it over to me." When it was my turn to speak to the group at the meeting I said to them, "I've signed so many IEP's, IPP's and IPT's that I feel I'm just about peed out."

I still had to sign a myriad of forms. I even was asked to fill out forms that would make it possible for me to become my son's legal guardian in case he might decide to get married or want a driver's license. I refused to become Carlton's legal guardian. I know I was probably wrong for doing that. I refused because everyone I dealt with on Carlton's behalf accepted my being his father as being legal without signing papers.

Laws making paperwork meant paper work leading to new laws. That was not a new phenomenon. It's been going on ever since we've opted on laws instead of common sense. My first experience of well intended legislation came when all the retarded citizens were to be deinstitutionalized. The intent was good; get the developmentally disabled backing into their own communities. Unfortunately, there was a lack of preparation for the facilities that would be receiving these people. Due to this lack of preparation many developmentally disabled persons and many parents were made to suffer through a long period of inadequate care and uncertainty.

In time, when facilities such as Hilldale developed plans to meet the needs of those living there, it was decided that large facilities must be more homelike. A homelike facility would be a more "normal" environment for the people living there. The word used to describe this new thinking was "normalization." The people living in the facility should have access to whatever was theirs. "Access" became the key to success. For Carlton this meant he would be able to get the things he needed whenever he wanted them. Carlton didn't realize he had any needs. He did, however, want everything he could get his hands on. Until access became the "in" thing, Carlton's closet and drawers were locked. He was given what he needed when the time was right. I was informed of access on one of my visits to Hilldale, almost as an apology. I was told there would be no more locked closets or drawers because locked closets and locked drawers were not normal. I was amazed at this turn of events. In my wildest imagination I couldn't see how unlocking drawers and closets would make Carlton normal. I tried to explain that Mimi and I were comfortable with locked closets and drawers because that way Carlton had a fifty fifty chance of retaining some of his possessions. Unlocking everything made closets and dressers open game to the more active residents who collected everything they could get their hands on. Unfortunately my concerns weren't within the law.

At one of our parent meetings I brought up the issue of what is normal for a seriously developmentally disabled person. The parents as a group thought there was nothing normal about their child and requested a meeting with the person or persons responsible for unlocking closets and drawers. A woman from State Licensing agreed to speak at our next meeting. At the meeting in an austere and professional manner, she tried to make us understand the reasoning of the powers that be. She didn't bother to visit the residents whose closets were being affected, and she didn't talk to any of the parents before hand. Instead she proceeded to show us the errors of our ways. She read us the rules and the state mandate that every individual in an institutional setting would have the same access to personal items as any other citizen of the state. Each resident would have his or her own desk and lamp and access to all personal toileting articles like tooth brush, toothpaste, soap and razors. I tried to explain to her that Carlton and the other residents didn't need a desk or a lamp. Having access to their own razors, soap and toothpaste would create chaos, slit throats and poor nutrition would surely follow. The well intentioned licensing woman looked at me, held firm and said "But it's the law and Hilldale must obey the law or be fined."

Letters were written as all of us saw the contradictions in this law as it pertained to our children living at Hilldale. Nothing changed. Inspectors from Licensing would come through and write up noncompliance after noncompliance. The parents suggested the cabinets be locked and the residents be given a key to the lock. This idea was quickly rejected because the residents couldn't use the keys. All our other suggestions were rejected without discussion. In time the people from licensing seemed to forget their rule. The closets and drawers were again locked. Keys were all over the place, available to nurses, aides, parents, friends and residents. Personal items were distributed as needed and other crises passed in the lives of the folks living at Hilldale.

After we got deinstitutionalization, normalization, and access out of the way, we were confronted with a new challenge "community awareness." Here again it was trial and error. Carlton and his friends at Hilldale only left Hilldale when parents picked them up for a home visit. Before being placed at Hilldale, these young persons were hidden away in State Hospitals. When they moved to community facilities deinstitutionalization became the buzzword. This was indeed a giant step in the normalization process. Even though the community facilities and the communities themselves weren't ready for these severely handicapped persons, the "System" decided that community awareness was necessary for the success of these community residential programs.

We began making the community aware of Hilldale by bringing in volunteers to play and sing with the residents. Once we had some volunteers, we started taking the residents on field trips. We found a few organizations in San Diego who would give us tickets to programs and events that were taking place in the area. They gave us tickets to circuses, baseball games, tennis matches, band competitions, parties for handicapped children, Christmas concerts, movies, puppet shows, museums, the zoo, Sea World and many other happenings. All we had to do was get the residents to the event. Sometimes we rented a bus, other times we used our own cars. We always needed one volunteer per resident so sometimes our group would be huge. We created quite a stir. The community really did become aware of us but not in the way the state had anticipated. Their awareness was similar to our awareness of the starving children in Somalia. The community knew these severely handicapped persons were there but they really didn't want to see them.

One time we went to Ringling Brothers Circus at the Sports Arena. We rented two buses to take forty four residents and volunteers. Just getting them all on the buses was a feat worthy of The Guinness Book of Records. Some were in wheel chairs, some were blind and some were oblivious to the world around them. For many it was their first bus ride.

When we got to the Sports Arena we unloaded and trudged into the arena and found our seats. The residents were overwhelmed by the size of the auditorium. Some were scared, others thrilled, some laughed, some yelled and some just sat and stared.

The show was about to begin and the arena went dark. All of a sudden the center of the arena came alive with light as the circus parade began. When those lights came on, one of our residents, Tony let out a howl you could hear all over the stadium. He started crying, and there was no way to comfort him. He was hysterical. We had to take him out. The people in our area looked at our group with utter contempt. Once outside Tony stopped crying. On another occasion at an Ice skating show at the arena, the same thing happened, the lights went out, the stage lights came on and Tony went berserk. We discovered a short time later that Tony's eyes were extremely sensitive to bright lights. Tony's problem was not discovered by a doctor, it was discovered by us. We decided not to take Tony to any more arena events.

As time went on the situation improved. We were able to go out to fast food restaurants, stores, movies and public events with just a few residents at a time. Behavior improved and people became used to seeing them around town. The community generally has accepted our sons and daughters. They fit in quite well now. The process of community awareness has evolved over the past twenty years. When I signed Carlton's IPP form, his program called for him to walk around his neighborhood for thirty minutes without exhibiting adverse behavior and calling undo attention to himself. For some reason that struck me as community awareness in reverse.

With deinstitutionalization, normalization, access and community awareness all in place a new buzzword, Age Appropriateness, came to the forefront. With age appropriateness parents found themselves between a rock and a hard place. We wanted the very best for our sons and daughters. Professionals that work with our children wanted the very best for them too. Unfortunately, the professionals think they know more about our children than we parents do. No one ever listens to parents or takes what they have to say seriously.

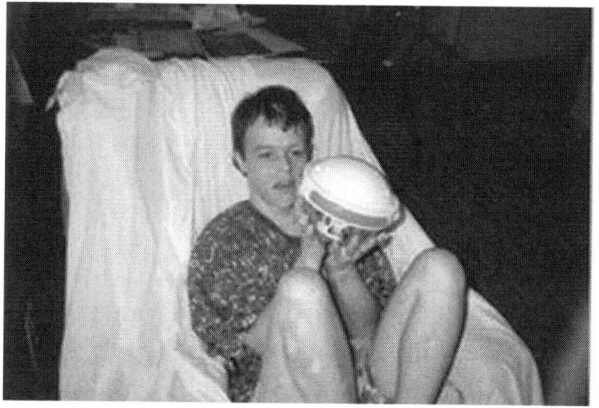

Carlton with a ball. He is in his 30's in this picture. You can see the changes in his skin form his Alopecia. He eventually lost all his hair and he looked great bald. It is how the family remembers him best.

Everything Carlton used or played with had to be age appropriate. This new dimension to Carlton's life style caused us a great deal of concern. We hadn't been able to figure out just what was appropriate for a thirty three year old adult male with the mind of a two or three year old child. Do you go by size or do you go by mental age? Parents tend to go by mental age, Professionals go by chronological age. Birthdays and Christmases cause much consternation.

When Mimi shopped for Colleen, Tom and Alicia, she got clothes and personal things for their enjoyment. Tom was into toys that flew, Colleen liked ceramic angels and Alicia liked anything that was rose colored. Carlton got clothes with his name written on them and an age appropriate toy.

AGE APPROPRIATE

By the time your son is thirty four years old, age appropriate things should be easy. Something for his car or house. New tools or something for his stereo. If he's a hunter a new gun, a fisherman a new pole or special plug. If he's a professional, we can give him something that will enhance his work, maybe a desk clock.

Carlton needed none of the above, so we looked for simple toys that are appropriate for a thirty four year old man-child. Every year he got a ball of some kind, not a rubber ball which wasn't age appropriate but a small toy ball that looked like a basketball, football or baseball. He loved spinning tops so we got him spinning tops but we kept them at home lest he got caught playing with an inappropriate plaything. We also gave him pull toys, wooden trains and multi colored spin toys. He thoroughly enjoyed playing with all those things.

Carlton left our home when he was eight. He had never left our family. Some of the residents at Hilldale lived with their parents and grandparents well into their twenties. If you raised a developmentally disabled child at home for twenty seven years, you deserve to be heard. If you raised your child at home for eight years you deserve to be heard. Both parents and professionals can make the system work if they just listen to one another.

When I wrote about age appropriateness in my monthly newsletter to the parents of the residents of Hilldale. I wrote;

"I had an opportunity to talk with Vickie, our recreation director. It has not been easy to come up with a recreation program for everyone living at Hilldale because some residents are so limited in what they can do. They want her to implement programs that are "age appropriate." This is a concept that drives me, as Carlton's father, up a wall! There are not a lot of activities a thirty year old such as Carlton can do, so rather than allowing him to enjoy some very simple tasks, he will probably do nothing. Maybe when you have the next IPP for your child you can mention you are willing to have him or her do any activity that might be fun, even if it might not be considered age appropriate. I'm sure some of you may tell me I'm crazy for holding my son back, but I feel he ought to be doing something that he could enjoy, even if it might look infantile."

I found out I wasn't alone when I got another parent's response in a letter a few weeks later:

Dear Carl

Once again procrastination has been my nemeses, and I don't have time to put in writing this letter that's been percolating in my mind ever since your April letter. It's this nonsense about "age appropriate materials" that prompts me to write. It is with major effort I stop this pen from scribbling the profound anger I feel at whoever dreamed up this insulting piece of hypocrisy! "age appropriate," indeed!! My son, Mark, was forty years old on the day of your May meeting-- and at his age, golf clubs would be appropriate! So would a bowling ball, or a new car! Maybe a nifty hand gun would be appropriate? Then rather than scratching his victims, this blind 40 year old could shoot them.

I do not care how old Mark is chronologically! If the sounds of a baby's rattle please him, he should have one! How dare anyone be so shallow as to think an age appropriate "toy" would improve the quality of his (or Carlton's) life? It seems to me an effort--- a very superficial one---to make these "adult-children" more visually- acceptable to those idealists who are embarrassed by reality! Please quote me--loudly--if it's ever possible

Betty

Carlton at 25 visiting home notice his favorite toy, a ball, is never far away

Christmas had again come and gone. Tom got a new turntable for his stereo and a warm flannel shirt and a propeller toy that will probably land on the roof. Colleen got a feather comforter for her bed and a beautiful ceramic angel. Alicia got chairs for her room, flannel sheets and a rose colored basket of soaps. Carlton got a new shirt, a fake soccer ball and a spin top that we didn't dare let out of the house. When Carlton came home, Mimi and I enjoyed seeing him play with it even though we might have been contributing to his eventual downfall in the world of the appropriate. One might say that after all these years Carlton had finally come out of the closet as age inappropriate. It's too bad his favorite toys couldn't have come out of the closet with him.

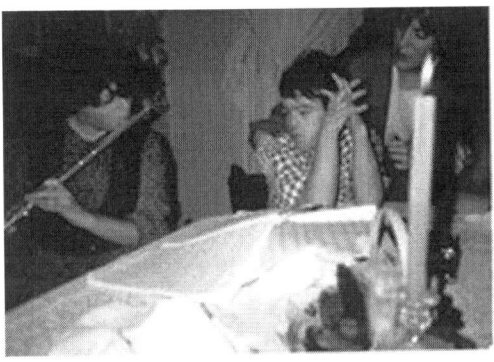

Colleen entertaining Carlton at Thanksgiving. Alicia is in the background.

In time cooler heads prevailed and age appropriate materials were individualized to meet the needs of the severely handicapped. Today no one seems to notice or care what a resident plays with. They are in programs that use materials and activities that are suited to their ability levels and life goes on. For developmentally disabled individuals life gets better every day.

BLUE RIBBON TASK FORCE

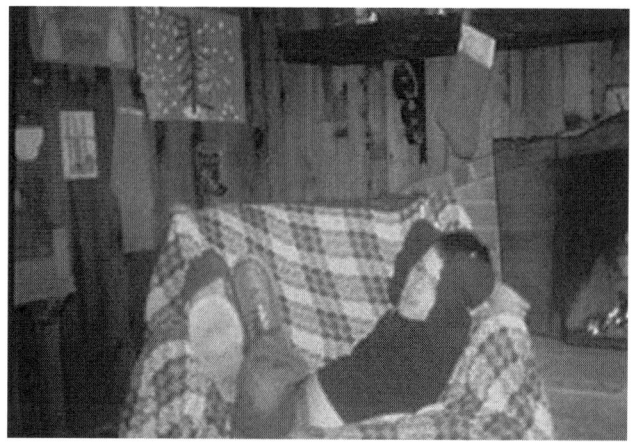

Carlton relaxing during a home visit in the 80's

In 1975 our world came crashing down around us. During the five years Carlton had lived at Hilldale the situation grew steadily worse. The care that was given our children was appalling. There wasn't enough help, the food was poor and the facility was not clean and smelled of urine and feces. Communication between parents and Hilldale was non existent. Adding insult to injury we were restricted from visiting our children except during regular visiting hours.

Because of the wretched situation, we had Carlton at home as often as possible. We cleaned him up, put decent clothes on him and fed him. When the time came to take him back to Hilldale, he didn't want to leave our house. When we arrived at the facility he resisted going in. The guilt and despair we felt was almost unbearable. We had no one to turn to. It seemed that those who were in positions to help us were advocating for Hilldale. We were alone.

Fortunately we had our parent group. Bad times were bringing the group closer together. We all wanted the best for our children. For some of the parents closing Hilldale was the only answer. Others insisted that Hilldale had to be cleaned up and operated in a caring way.

One particular disciplinary method that concerned us was the "time out" room. This "time out" room was a dark closet where residents would be confined when they misbehaved or didn't do what a staff member wanted them to do. The "time out" would help the person understand the errors of his or her ways. Therefore, the offensive behavior wouldn't be repeated because the culprit would realize that the behavior was unacceptable.

Mimi complained about this mistreatment to the owner, William Bauer. She told him that she would be frightened if she were placed in a dark closet. It would be even more frightening to the severely handicapped persons in his care. He replied "Now, now Mrs. Smith, you sleep in a dark room don't you?" Mimi was furious. She told him he was very cruel. She did not set foot in Hilldale for over a year.

I continued to visit Hilldale at least three times a week because we were doing Carlton's laundry and having him home as often as possible. Carlton was diapered by the staff although he was sixteen and easily trainable. Frequently when I picked up his laundry, dirty diapers hadn't even been rinsed out. We threw out more of his smelly clothes than we washed. Other parents complained about the appearance of the clothes that were put on their sons and daughters. White clothes become dingy gray, color clothes faded and all the clothes smelled. Our complaints were never acted upon.

Carlton and Mimi at one of his favorite places the kitchen table.

I found a portable potty in Carlton's room one day. When I asked why it was there, they said that Carlton's roommate was being potty trained. I told them I didn't like it in his room because Carlton could get to the contents of the potty and become ill. I was assured that the contents were emptied immediately and the potty cleaned. Time after time I found the potty filled with urine and feces.

My only recourse was to call Licensing and report the situation. A person from Licensing showed up to investigate my complaint but it only made matters worse. Now instead of correcting an obvious flaw, they avoided me or announced that I was at the door before they would let me in.

Food was another area of concern. Residents living at Hilldale who went to programs during the week took their lunches with them. Carlton and some other residents went to St. Madeline Sophies. The staff knew Mimi and me and would tell us when the residents of Hilldale showed up ill-clothed, smelling bad or with unacceptable lunches. We in turn pressured Hilldale to improve. One time the custodian called to tell me the milk Hilldale students had was outdated and sour. I called Hilldale to tell them. Their reaction was to get angry at St. Madeline Sophies for telling me. We began putting the Hilldale lunches in our freezers as evidence in case we had to verify our complaints.

The parents complained about dirty linen, odors, dirty clothes, dirty residents, poor health care, lack of programming, untrained help and just the general poor treatment of our sons and daughters. Our parent meetings were the only outlet for our frustrations. The parents were angry and wanted something done.

We soon discovered we were not alone. Complaints were coming to the County Board of Supervisors about facilities throughout San Diego County. Some complaints came from relatives of persons living in nursing homes, Staff at the facilities complained that they were asked to do more than was humanly possible. Still other complaints came from families like ours with children placed in facilities like Hilldale. The California Public Interest Research Group (CALPIRG) a watchdog organization began looking into the nursing home situation. They found many conditions similar to those at Hilldale in facilities throughout the county and published their findings.

Captain Sticky and radio personality Bill Balance

Then Captain Sticky appeared on the scene. He was a self-proclaimed cape crusader. Captain Sticky wore a Superman costume and drove around town in the "Stickymobile." His Stickymobile was a large black and red town car with turrets and chrome bugle horns and all kinds of trinkety decorations. He thrived on peanut butter and jelly sandwiches. He weighed close to three hundred pounds. In his superman outfit, he was something to behold. Nursing home abuse was his cause in 1975. He and a number of activists would picket a targeted nursing facility; enter if they could and write down all the faults they observed. It was only natural that the newspapers, alerted in advance, covered a story that centered on an obese Superman, driving an obnoxious automobile defending the helpless.

He learned I was president of the parents group at Hilldale, the only group actively involved as advocates for persons living in any kind of nursing homes at that time. He called me to see if he could convince us to march with him. He believed the only way to change the situation at Hilldale was to make the public aware of it. If the parents would picket and march through the facility venting their frustration, change would happen. He asked me if he could come to our next meeting to try and convince us to march with him.

I explained to him that we shared his concerns, but the parents were not activists and would feel threatened in such a roll. Most were afraid that their child would be moved back to a state hospital if they spoke out. They did not want to rock the boat. Just thinking of having their child move back frightened them, knowing the distance would make it impossible for them to visit their child.

Captain Sticky had a difficult time understanding our reservations. He wanted a better situation for our kids and so did we. But we feared with his approach, change might come but our sons and daughters would be gone.

Captain Sticky continued to march on one nursing facility after another. He especially targeted the Casablanca Corp (the corporation that owned Hilldale), which seemed to be the worst offender. Captain Sticky tried to enter Hilldale on one of his nursing home raids. Mr. Bauer barred him and threatened him with police action. Undaunted, Captain Sticky pursued his quest.

In order to get to the bottom of the charges against nursing facilities the county established a "Blue Ribbon Task Force on Nursing Homes" Captain Sticky, Superman costume and all, was chosen to be one of task force members. People like him are needed to give public apathy a wake-up call.

Looking back the whole incident was a time of great change, a change of attitude, a change in relationship between parents and people charged with the care of their children and finally a change in the care provided by nursing facilities. The change that took place can best be described through a series of letters and newspaper articles written at the time. It began when Casablanca made headlines:

Casa Blanca Claims CALPIRG Irresponsible

Probers Banned From Nursing Chain

The Casa Blanca chain of nursing homes, including two in the East County, has been ordered to refuse entry to members of the California Public Interest Research Group (CALPIRG), which is conducting an investigation of skilled nursing facilities in the county.

The order by Casa Blanca chairman William Bauer was issued following visits by CALPIRG members to the Lemon Grove Convalescent Center at 8351 Broadway, Lemon Grove, and the Madison Convalescent Center at 1391 E. Madison Ave., El Cajon.

CALPIRG director Dan Franklin accused Casa Blanca officials of trying to hinder the investigation by what he said were "crude attempts at intimidation and harrassment."

According to Franklin, the executive vice president of the nursing home chain, Henry Swambat, sent a letter to the dean of student affairs at University of California at San Diego complaining that CALPIRG volunteers conducted "surreptitious, illegal entries" and spread "unfounded horror story tales'' regarding the visits to the two East County facilities.

A majority of CALPIRG's funding is provided by student funds at UCSD.

In response to CALPIRG's charges, Swambat today called the organization an "irresponsible group" whose tactics and manners are "very, very unprofessional."

He said Casa Blanca, which has nine facilities in its chain, does not recognize CALPIRG as a proper investigative body and that its volunteers have displayed unprofessional conduct at other nursing facilities in the county.

According to Franklin, the visits to the two nursing homes were part of CALPIRG's study of issues relating to long-term care facilities. The purpose, he said, is to generate proposals to ensure high quality nursing care. CALPIRG's final report is expected to be released this summer.

According to Alan Kremen, a student at UCSD and coordinator of the project, volunteers have been "very pleased" with the cooperation displayed from almost all the facilities that have been visited.

Kremen said that he and two other CALPIRG members observed several conditions at Lemon Grove Convalescent Center on April 10 which appeared to be violations of state health department regulations. Swambat denies the facilities are in violation of the regulations.

Swambat's assertion is supported by Mitchell Kotula, assistant district administrator in the facilities licensing section of the State Health Dept. in San Diego.

Kotula said this morning that a field inspection by his office was made April 11 at the request of Assemblyman Bob Wilson's office. His inspector, a representative of Wilson's and CALPIRG people went along on the inspection, which Swambat said was unannounced.

"The CALPIRG people simply had a misunderstanding of what the state regulations were. Our inspector found no violations," Kotula said.

> Later, Kremen said, Casa Blanca officials contacted officials at UCSD and San Diego State University, which also provides funds for CALPIRG, in an attempt to halt the investigation.
>
> Franklin said he asked for an apology from Casa Blanca officials during a meeting with them April 29, but was refused, and that Bauer, the chairman of the nursing home chain, then ordered his facilities to refuse entry to anyone from CALPIRG in the future.
>
> Kremen said that, throughout the investigation, CALPIRG has "scrupulously avoided sensationalism and has been committed to making no allegations public which could not be proven."
>
> Swambat claimed that CALPIRG volunteers displayed unprofessional conduct at other nursing facilities which Casa Blanca officials had contacted.

The first thing the task force did was to ask for input from the community. It was flooded with letters from parents with children at Hilldale. Both representatives from Casablanca and parents from Hilldale were at each meeting of the task force. During the course of the proceedings, both groups were asked to speak before the committee.

When the Blue Ribbon Task Force asked for input, Mimi and I each wrote the task force immediately. The letters follow:

Dear Mrs. Helton

I am a parent of a developmentally disabled child who has been placed at Hilldale. For the past few years I have worked to make parent input an important part of Hilldale's program and care policy. I have been instrumental in setting up the Family and Friends of Hilldale, a parent group. During this past two years I have become very frustrated over the role of parent of a child in residential care. As a parent I want to be involved in my child's progress. I want to know what he is doing, what he is learning and what is effective in making him function at the level where he is. I know I cannot have Carlton home because the care he needs is beyond the ability of my family. Still he is my child and I am concerned, so what do I do? First I wanted to work with other parents who had common concerns. To do this I formed a parent group. We met and found our concerns were personal and focused on our own child. As a group we were not functioning. A concern of mine might not necessarily be a concern of another parent. We regrouped. We set up a parent group that we felt would be meaningful, a group that would open communication among parents, staff and administration.

We developed a constitution that would make us a viable group. . We felt by doing this we could change the facility attitude from -leave us alone- to one of cooperation between parent and facility. After two years it seems clear to me that this was the wrong approach. It was wrong because parents have no legal rights concerning policy and program. Hilldale pays attention to Regional Center, Licensing and CSS. The parents are just another group that they don't have to bother with so they don't. I can't blame them for that. As a parent, however, it is very frustrating. If Regional Center, Licensing or CSS says something is alright and I as a parent disagree, that's tough. If I, as a parent, say this is how my child learns best, but Regional Center, Licensing or CSS disagree I lose. It's difficult to have every concern minimized because no one is required to listen to me. In other words "you are only a Parent" is the message that comes across loud and clear.

What can be done to relieve this situation and make community placement meaningful for the children as well as the parent? When parents are able to be heard their concerns can realistically be integrated into successful programs of community care. I feel you can't legislate trust but some kind of parent rights can be ordained as part of a facility policy in order to receive a resident. Parents should be informed of a facility's policies. Parents should be informed of their rights as parents. Parents should be able to be heard without going to Licensing, Regional Center, or CSS. As it now stands parents are asked to share their concerns only with the site administrator. That's fine if you can get satisfaction. If not, you are supposed to accept it as just one of those things that only effects your child while we, the organization are thinking of all our clients, so forget it.

I see the parents as valuable allies to the facility and all the involved agencies. Yes, they did give their children up for reasons known only to themselves, reasons that are many and reasons that are valid. They are still parents, however, and as such are at least as important as nurses, aides and administrators who work at these facilities. They do not love their children less because they are institutionalized. They are not ashamed of their children. They are not happy because this situation exists. They are only parents.

In conclusion I see more responsibility has to be taken by the various agencies to integrate the parents into the system. This is indeed a new challenge as our children are being returned to our communities. For this I thank the Lord. I only wish and pray that I could be more a part of formulating Carlton's future.

Sincerely
Carl F Smith

Mimi wrote a more personal letter. She was still upset with her run in with Mr. Bauer. She had to be heard by someone so she wrote to the Blue Ribbon Task Force.

Dear Task Force Members

Sixteen years ago when a doctor told me that my first born was retarded, I felt pain, grief and love. Since that time my husband and family have had many joys and sorrows as we continue to grow and become the full persons I believe God wants us to be.

Since our son Carlton has been living at Hilldale I have seen little improvement in his general care. When he came home for visits he was not clean, wrapped in diapers, (although toilet trained) had a towel that reached to his knees pinned around his neck, his shirt and pants were pinned together with large safety pins. Thanks to Sister Ellen who worked at St. Madeline Sophies at that time the towel was removed. When she went to work at Hilldale programs of toilet training and hand washing were begun.

When I went into Hilldale, Carlton and the other children never had shoes on. One day when I asked for Carlton's shoes and socks, it took at least twenty minutes and an aide to locate a pair of socks. Thanks to Nancy Seppella, our outstanding social worker, the children now wear shoes and socks.

When my husband and I wanted to take Carlton to a doctor of our choice, Mrs. Mumford called me into her office. She was upset with our decision. At one time she told me to take Carlton out of Hilldale if I was unhappy. Mrs. Mumford and Mr. Bauer have used this statement as a threat to me and other parents.

It is unfortunate that parents haven't been heard as we've tried to build an open, trusting relationship with Mr. Bauer and Mrs. Mumford. The pain and grief which I felt sixteen years ago when we learned that Carlton was retarded is so minute compared to the utter desolation I feel now. Mr. Bauer told our parent group on Monday evening that we as parents do not have a say in programs that the agencies and he decide what is okay for his clients at Hilldale. He brought up the "time out" room, saying the Task Force Committee is blowing things out of proportion. In my opinion Hilldale's "closeting" of its residents is outrageous!

My husband, who works with disturbed children, told Mr. Bauer that he felt the parents should have been informed about the room and given a choice on the use of this treatment for their child. Properly used by well informed people, "time out" rooms can be effective tools for modifying a child's behavior. Mr. Bauer said that a psychologist told the staff to use the room and they had to because he was an authority. When I said, "Mr.

Bauer, not a dark room!" he replied, "you sleep in a dark room, don't you?" I told him, "that's so unkind, Oh Mr. Bauer that's cruel!" I left the meeting.

My hopes of ever having any understanding from Mr. Bauer and Mrs. Mumford are gone. I now know that management, CSS and Regional Center come first. I know my place as the D.D. system sees it, I just can't accept it.

I can accept the fact that my son is retarded. However, as a mother, I have accepted the responsibility for his growth and development, limited though they may be. By placing Carlton at Hilldale, I had hoped to share with the administration the responsibility for my son, in an atmosphere of mutual trust. I feel that they cannot accept this mutual relationship.

Every effort I have made to share openly with them regarding my concerns for my son's welfare have been met with distrust and fear that I am infringing on "their territory." Mr. Bauer has not only minimized my concern regarding my son, but is trying to discredit the effort of the Task Force. He does not seem to understand the philosophy of public responsibility which we all share in a free society. I am at a loss as to how to awaken Mr. Bauer's conscience and sense of awareness and responsibility toward the residents at Hilldale, their families and the public.

Sincerely yours
Muriel A Smith

Shortly after Mimi wrote her letter, she was asked to speak to the task force. She was interviewed by the panel for over an hour. Her testimony changed the focus of the hearings from the investigation of nursing homes to an investigation of Casablanca Corp. Mimi was interviewed for TV and the local paper. Our plight was becoming well publicized. Maybe Captain Sticky had been right.

Here is the transcript of the San Diego Union article by Jon Funabiki (see image that follows):

Retarted Boy's Mother Despairs Policy

CHULA VISTA—Mrs. Mimi Smith's voice tremored with anger and frustration as she described yesterday the "utter desolation" of being shut off from her 16-year-old mentally retarded son's life in a La Mesa nursing home.

"Every effort I have made to share openly with them (the nursing home) my concerns for my son's welfare has been met with mistrust and fear that I am infringing on their territory." Mrs. Smith told a county investigative panel on nursing homes.

'UTTER DESOLATION'

"The pain and grief which I felt 16 years ago when we learned that Carlton had Down's Syndrome (mongolism) is so minute to the utter desolation I feel now."

The twelve member task force was formed by the county Board of Supervisors to hear and investigate complaints about nursing homes and to recommend possible reforms. About 80 persons attended yesterday's public hearing at City Hall, where the first hour was consumed by the testimony of Mrs. Smith, a San Diego substitute teacher.

Mrs. Smith told the panel she had seen improvements in Carlton's care since placing him in the nursing home about three years ago, but there still is no communication between families, staff and administration.

'HAVE NO SAY'

Parents have been told that they 'have no say' in the planning of programs and methods of treatment used, she said, and staff members that work closest with the children are instructed to refer parents' questions to the administration rather than to answer them.

She said she accepted as a mother the responsibility for her son's growth and development—"limited though it may be"—and placed him in the nursing home hoping "to share with the administration this responsibility for my son, in an atmosphere of mutual trust."

But, she said "I feel that they cannot accept this mutual relationship."

TASK FORCE HEAD

Mrs. Maggie Helton, a retired school nurse, and chairman of the task force asked Mrs. Smith whether she felt the nursing was "closing you out of your son's life."

"Yes" Mrs. Smith replied nodding several times.

Mrs. Smith's son is a patient at the Hilldale Convalescent Center, but Mrs. Helton said that her panel during its three previous public hearings hears similar complaints about other nursing homes as well.

The frustration of feeling 'cut off' form their child's life is a common complaint expressed in the testimony of parents said Mrs. Helton. The same has proved true of family members speaking of the care of elderly persons in nursing homes she said.

'KNOW WHAT IS BEST'

"The facility says 'We know what's best for your child—don't tell us what to do'" says Mrs Helton. "That's the feeling the parents have."

"Many times the child must be hospitalized and concerned parents like Mrs. Smith don't want to be cut off from their child and what their care is." Mrs. Helton said.

After Mimi's day of pleading her case, many parents from the Hilldale parent's group were asked to appear before the panel. Each one verified the concerns put forward by Mimi and added some things they felt demanded attention.

The last parent to testify to the task force was Marion Snow. She had two severely handicapped daughters at Fairview State Hospital. One of her daughters had lived at Hilldale. Due to Mrs. Snow's outspoken activism Hilldale managed to get her to have her daughter transferred back to Fairview State Hospital. Mrs. Snow was a true advocate for persons with severe handicaps. She was the most informed and the most outspoken parent in our group. Immediately after her visit to the task force, Mr. Bauer sent a letter to all the parents explaining how those testifying before the Blue Ribbon Task Force were doing a grave injustice to Hilldale and their children.

CASA BLANCA
Convalescent Homes

Dear Parent

At the January 5 Public Hearing of the San Diego Task Force on Nursing Homes, Mrs. Marion Snow mother of a former resident of Hilldale Convalescent Center, testified that:

1) *Community nursing homes are failing to provide adequate concern and levels of care for developmentally disabled clients;*

2) *Regional Center has proven itself ineffective in its legislated role of D.D. advocate;*

3) *Therefore, the Task Force should support the only alternative that she has found satisfactory - namely, the return of D.D. clients to State Hospitals, such as Fairview.*

Casa Blanca, on the other hand, supports-- along with the State and many parents--the current practice of serving developmentally disabled in their own local communities. We feel we have been successful in improving levels of care substantially at our three D.D. Client Care units during the last few years, even at the very restrictive reimbursement rates paid by the State for such care.

Further, contrary to Ms. Snow's testimony, we have found Dr. Peterson, other officials and staff of Regional Center to be particularly strong advocates for their D.D. clients---advocates who have been persistent in their follow-up and requests on behalf of their clients.

If you agree with us, we feel it is extremely important at this time for you to write Chairperson Helton of the task force expressing your support of community care and Regional Center.---on the other hand, you feel, like Ms. Snow that your child is better served in State institutions, I am sure Task Force members would similarly like to hear from you.

Because of her twenty years of activity in the area of mental retardation, Task Force members accepted Ms. Snow's presentation as expert testimony and, accordingly, invited her to sit in on one of their final January 14, 21, and 28 workshops at which they will formulate their recommendations to our County Board of Supervisors.

Unless other parents, guardians, physicians, and individuals and groups concerned with the welfare of the developmentally disabled "come forth" in writing to this Task Force NOW- the members may interpret Ms. Snow's opinions as representative of all parents and recommend the return and placement of D.D. clients in State, rather than community facilities. We encourage you to let your wishes be known. Ms. Helton's mailing address is noted below.

Sincerely Yours
CASA BLANCA CONVALESCENT HOMES
Wm. J Bauer President

Mimi and I didn't think Mr. Bauer's letter to the parents painted a true picture of what Marion said in her testimony. We didn't hear her say that under any circumstance all D.D. persons should be sent back to State Hospitals. The letter did get Mimi to write the Task force in defense of Marion.

Dear Ms. Helton

On January 5. I attended the meeting that Mrs. Snow spoke about her experiences with Hilldale Convalescent Home. At no time did she say that all D.D. clients should be returned to State Hospitals. I thought I heard Mrs. Snow say that Hilldale was not meeting the needs of clients, parents and their staff. Isn't that the question your task force is asking and looking into in San Diego.

To me, Casa Blanca's letter to the parent on January 8 seems to be another scare tactic used to shut parents up. In his letter Mr. William J Bauer said, "Because of her twenty years of activity in the area of mental retardation, task force members accepted Ms. Snow's presentation as expert testimony." Fine, I hope you will, since Mrs. Snow has been active in the field of retardation because of her children. Her aim is better conditions for all retarded people. Mr. Bauer's letter upsets me because parents who weren't at the hearing might believe it and consider Mrs. Snow a troublemaker. How does Mr. Bauer know how any members of your task force accepted testimony until you sum up your findings?

Personally I don't see how Casa Blanca can be allowed to continue operations after hearing the devious manner in which Mr. Bauer operates his nursing homes.

Since the Hilldale Facility Committee is the only way our Parent Group has to communicate with Mrs. Mumford and Hilldale, disbanding it tells us again that they don't want our input.

Really I don't see how our D.D. people can be served by an organization run by Mr. William Bauer. He says unkind things to parents and uses our emotions and love for our children against us. If the State grants more money to community care, I hope the money will have to be used to pay staff and provide useful programs for the retarded.

As for my son Carlton I don't want him placed out of San Diego, but there isn't any alternative to Mr. Bauer's facilities. It's my dream that someday parents and facility will have honest communications. A difficult situation can then become a joy instead of a battle.

Wishing you beautiful things while you continue with your task force challenge.

Sincerely
Muriel A Smith

The hearings were finally over. With all the bad publicity Hilldale was getting the tension between the parents and the facility was acute. It was so bad that the director of the Regional Center, Dr. Peterson arranged a meeting with some of our parents, himself, Mr. Bauer and the director of CSS, Don Cogbburn. Not much came out of the meeting. Mr. Bauer offered to buy a new washing machine if that would make us happy. He said he hoped that would get us off his back for a while. It didn't.

An uneasy peace settled over Hilldale. Now that everyone had said their piece, we became necessary enemies. We needed Hilldale and Hilldale needed us. The parents were concerned that we might have gone too far. We wanted to be supportive of the people who worked at Hilldale, but they weren't' allowed to talk to us. We saw the stress Hilldale was under. We knew the staff was working hard to do well for our kids. We also knew that Hilldale was under staffed and under funded. We wanted to work with Hilldale to gain more staff and more funds. The administration of Hilldale didn't see things the way we did. They thought we were out to get them so they withdrew from us. They did everything their way whether we liked it or not. Something had to be done to relieve the tension. I wrote what I hoped would be the final curtain on this difficult time. I sent copies to Hilldale, the County Board of Supervisors, CSS, Regional Center and Licensing.

Dear Sirs,

As president of the Families of Hilldale I have been asked to write you on behalf of the parents of the residents of Hilldale Convalescent Center. During the past few months the parents of the Hilldale residents have been very much concerned about our children and the concept of community care for the developmentally disabled. At our last meeting we discussed our concerns openly and as a group decided to write this letter concerning our feelings about community care.

We all feel that having our children in the community is one of the best things that has happened in our children's' treatment program. It brings our children back home where we as parents can visit and have them home at more frequent intervals without traveling hundreds of miles to a State Hospital. We can watch our children grow and develop and be an integral part of our families.

During the recent hearings Hilldale seemed to play a central role. I and the parents feel this is due to our great concern for the well being of our children. Many things were said, some good, some bad. We're sure all were spoken with concern for the children who reside there. We were confused about the purpose of the task force. We received communications from Casa Blanca and we read many things in the newspapers. We seemed to be in the middle of something we didn't fully understand. Each time we received or read a communication we became more concerned about the future of community care and the future of our children.

As a group we highly commend Hilldale and the staff for the job they are doing. The care and love they offer our children is superior in light of the conditions that we, as parents, feel are very unfair. These conditions are the lack of funds that are so necessary for meeting the needs of the developmentally disabled. They are required to have twenty four hour a day nursing care for our children for less than twenty dollars a day. Due to this lack of funds the pay scale for the staff at Hilldale is inadequate compared to any health care service I can find. This causes a turnover of between 300 and 400 percent per year. Our children need consistency and this change of staff certainly has a poor effect on them. Developmentally Disabled individuals need trained help. This type of help is impossible to obtain at minimum wage. When the minimum wage was raised and food prices rose the dollar funding amount remained the same. How can care improve when monies just aren't being provided.

The State seems satisfied with community care because it is a lot cheaper than the State Hospital System. This is unrealistic because doing the job cheaper is not always doing the job right. Hilldale is doing the job *but it is unfair to see what is expected of the aides and nurses with the staffing that now exists.*

I wish each of you could visit Hilldale when the residents are getting ready for school or activity programs. You would see what the staff is up against. We parents know they are doing the best they can. We want them to do better but that will take more staff and more staff means more money. We feel the county as well as the state should encourage community care and assure its success with realistic funding.

Again, we are extremely happy to have our children in the community. We feel Hilldale and its staff are doing the best job they can possibly do under the circumstances. We feel trained staff are a necessity for a program's continuity. We feel to realistically make community care what it can ultimately be, demands adequate funding from all levels of government. With these things in mind consistency in program and optimum care can indeed be a reality.

Sincerely
Carl F Smith

The letter helped. Slowly people began talking to one another again. The State put a pilot program at Hilldale that enabled them to increase their staff and receive extra program money. The care was noticeably enriched; the residents looked better, smelled better, had more programs and were happier. Hilldale took all the credit for the improvements but we parents knew we had been the agents of change It didn't matter who claimed the credit, we got what we wanted all along, a better environment for our sons and daughters.

I did get a letter from the County acknowledging my letter. I never heard what happened to the task force. Mr. Bauer paid a fine for making illegal contributions to a politician. Mrs. Snow became the president of the parents group at Fairview State Hospital. The Families and Friends of Hilldale still meet once a month trying to help Hilldale any way we can. If anything stands out in my mind about that whole sorry episode it would have to be the Hilldale parents and Captain Sticky. To sum it up:

For parents--When parents band together for the good of their children, there is no more powerful group in the world.

For activists like Captain Sticky--When the going gets ridiculous, the ridiculous get going.

SANTA CLAUS

Tom and I in the front yard of our home in San Diego. I am dressed as Santa on my way to a Christmas celebration at Hilldale

The parents at Hilldale decided to sponsor a Christmas party for the residents at a time when I was the neighborhood rent-a-Santa. You would think, with four children, I would have remembered the Santa Clauses of old, the ones who were mutilated by Carlton and Alicia. No! Tradition said Santa was a part of our Christmas. Carlton was part of our family living at Hilldale. Our family tradition would now carry over to Hilldale. My whole perception of Santa Claus changed when I became Santa to the severely handicapped.

No matter what you do with severely handicapped persons, whether it's teaching them, playing with them, eating with them or being Santa to them, it is an experience far different from what one anticipates. Our first Christmas party at Hilldale proves the point.

There were three rooms at Hilldale large enough for fifteen to forty residents. The Recreation Director had thirty residents waiting for Santa in the large dining room and fourteen waiting in each of the other two. Before the party, parents wrapped gifts for the residents, coloring books, socks, toys, dolls, shaving soap, or similar small thing that they could open. Each gift had a resident's name on it. At the party, Santa would visit the three rooms and give each resident his or her gift. Naturally, Santa didn't know who every resident was so an aide would point out the recipient and Santa would hand the gift to him or her. It looked foolproof on paper.

The day arrived. Parents arrived with plates of cookies and presents for their child. One parent brought a magnificent ice cream cake. I arrived early to get into my Santa outfit. Now all I had to do was go in and pass out the presents.

I started my tour in the dining room with bells jingling and a jolly, "Ho, Ho, Ho!" This was the first time many of the residents had seen Santa. They didn't know what to make of my bells, red suit and white beard. The only real reaction I got was from a girl named Erin. When I danced in, Erin was terrified. She disappeared under her chair as if there was an earthquake drill.

Taken aback but undaunted, I hopped around from one resident to another repeating "Ho, Ho, Ho and Merry Christmas. Still I got no reaction. I was sure the presents would save the day. I grabbed a gift and Ho Hoed "Merry Christmas John T!" the tag read I looked at the aide and asked, "Which one is John T?" She said she was new and didn't know who John T. was either. I discovered there were only two aides at the party who had been working at Hilldale for more than two weeks.

When we finally got the gifts distributed, we realized no one was able to open their gift. Parents, aides and Santa had to open each present and give it to the resident. He or she in turn looked at the gift, held it for a moment and then in many cases threw it on the floor. It was a sight to behold, a trash collector's dream come true.

After I escaped from the chaos of the gift openings I visited the residents who were confined to their beds. By the time I finished these visitations my Santa suit felt like a sauna. I changed and returned to the party.

I thought the Santa visit had been well conceived until I returned to the refreshment phase of the party. It had taken Santa so long to pass out the presents, the ice cream cake was beginning to melt and the residents were trying to eat melting ice cream cake. Aides were picking up presents to keep them from being soaked by the dripping ice cream. Wrapping paper was everywhere. The cook was passing out cookies. Some of the residents were moving toward the undefended ice cream cake and trays of cookies. It was a scene from Dante's Inferno.

We thought a nice conventional Christmas party would add a bit of joy to the routine lives of the residents. It was definitely a break from the normal routine. Instead of the Christmas party we had anticipated, we had created a mess. As usual we learned from our mistakes.

Christmas parties at Hilldale changed over the years. A more realistic Santa took over for me. We never had another ice cream cake. Nowadays we mark the gifts "Boy" or "Girl" so Santa has an easier time distributing them. Each resident also receives a larger gift like a jogging suit, a comforter, a jacket or some kind of fitness apparatus.

Santa talks to each resident. He touches them and they touch him. Erin likes Santa now. Many of the residents respond to Santa with a smile, a giggle or a joyous grin. Some still just stare through him. The parties are more sedate with Santa Claus, Christmas carols, cookies and punch. A new parent brought real gooey cupcakes one year bringing back vivid memories of the ice cream cake.

I always look forward to Christmas. It's not all Santa Claus, but Santa's a significant part of it. He seems to be able to break down barriers and let us be children again. For the residents of Hilldale he is something different once a year. I like to believe they look forward to seeing him. They don't always show it, but I see it in my heart.

CHURCH

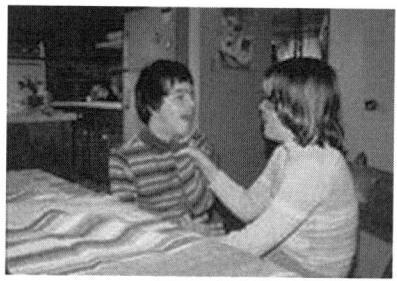

Carlton and Alicia. Carlton is about 17 Alicia is about 12. No matter how old their brother got he remained a constant source of fun to his siblings. He loved to play and laugh and just be with his family

Religion has always been a vital part of our lives. Mimi and I were raised Catholic. Throughout our lives we've remained faithful to our church. Six weeks after Carlton was baptized in the hospital by one of the nuns, we had a formal christening at our little church in Crestline. He wore the same christening gown his great grandmother had worn at her christening. Until Colleen was born, we took him to church every Sunday. Through the years we frequently were angry with God for all the roadblocks placed in our way because of Carlton. More often, however, we prayed for guidance and help for the ability to care for him.

When Carlton was placed out of our home, we stopped worrying about his spiritual growth. If any minister came to the facility or the hospital to recruit Carlton, it was all right with us. If Mrs. Belleheumer, his foster mother, wanted to take him to her church that was okay too. Our faith led us to believe that Carlton like Christ was a perfect human. While we struggle to earn eternal happiness, Carlton found it without even trying.

We never considered religion and its relationship to developmentally disabled persons until Carlton was placed at Hilldale. There were no church programs at Hilldale and as far as organized religion was concerned severely handicapped people did not exist. They were not included in church schools or church services.

There were people, however, from various religious congregations who went out of their way to make the parents and their handicapped child a part of their faith. Some offered to baby sit, some started religious classes and some invited them to their service.

One Baptist Church sent a bus to Hilldale every Sunday to pick up residents and staff who wanted to go to a two hour service and religious class prepared especially for them. The Home of Guiding Hands, a large residential facility founded by the Lutheran Church, had a full time chaplain, Reverend Anderson. Whenever a church, no matter the denomination, had a religious service or celebration that could be enhanced by the presence of severely handicapped people, they called the Reverend Anderson and he would be there with ten or twelve of his residents. The severely handicapped, because of their innocence, were exceptional models for any congregation. They always sang and responded with appropriate "Amens" during the service.

Carlton's attended St. Madeline Sophies' day program. It was under the direction of a Catholic nun, Sister Maxine Kraemer and was open to any developmentally disabled child that was in need of an educational program. Sisters purpose was not in converting these handicapped persons to the Catholic Church (the church didn't seem to want them to begin with. St. Madeline Sophie's was centered on faith in God. It was her ministry.

Sister asked if we would like Carlton to receive his First Communion and Confirmation. Mimi and I talked it over and decided it would be meaningless to Carlton so we said, "No". We discussed our decision with Sister and with our parish priest. We felt Carlton would spit out the Host if he didn't like it. Confirmation was a commitment to be actively involved in the faith. In either case, we saw a contradiction. They suggested that Carlton's reception of the sacrament would be good for the community even if Carlton didn't understand. We felt that might be true, but we stuck to our decision.

Confirmation at St. Madeline Sophie was an important day for Sister Kraemer and for some of the higher functioning persons who were being confirmed. As the bishop came down the aisle, the Knights of Columbus, dressed in their formal attire, black uniforms with large feather headdresses and swords, formed an honor guard. Somehow Carlton managed to snatch one of the Knight's sword. Carlton is tough to disarm when he gets his hands on anything. With my help, the Knight got his sword back. However, in the process, he almost lost his feathered hat to Carlton. The Knight finished the ceremony clutching his sword and keeping his eye on every retarded person in his vicinity.

The Bishop spoke to each Confirmee. Some sat on his lap, some saluted, and some enjoyed being touched by a famous person. The innocence of the people being confirmed moved us all. I'm sure some felt that this was a big step in the church's acceptance of developmentally disabled persons. As the service ended, Mimi andI I still felt we had made the right decision. Carlton seemed to get more out of his confrontation with the Knight over the sword and feathered hat than he did out of the service.

I have worked to gain support for the developmentally disabled and for those who work with them within the church. I have spoken at many parishes about Madeline Sophie's and the developmentally disabled in order to create awareness in the diocese. I encouraged the parishes to offer financial help as well as prayers for this segment of the population. Many parishioners came up to me after Mass and sought more information. Some did not know anything like St. Madeline Sophie's existed. Some knew someone who had a retarded child, and some were interested in learning more about retardation.

I also served on the board of Noah's Home, a complex of group homes serving about fifty higher functioning developmentally disabled persons. Sister Catherine Jennings who founded Noah's Home, captained it since its inception. Sister Jennings, like Sister Kraemer, spends many hours raising funds so that Noah's Home can meet the needs of those placed there. Today Noah Homes is a showpiece: housing, gardens, horses, theater groups, and transportation for all the residents living there. More and more people have come to know the developmentally disabled through Sister Jennings and Sister Kraemer. These people, in turn, help spread the word. In time, acceptance was no longer be our goal - integration was.

CHURCH

Jean Vanier, a Catholic layman, visited San Diego for a workshop on his program for the developmentally disabled. Vanier established l'Arche Communities, small communities or homes for disabled people throughout Europe, Canada, and the United States. L'Arche are communities of four to six people living together. One or two of the members are not handicapped and serve as mentors for all living there. The households develop as a family unit. They eat, play, pray and work together. While Vanier was working in a mental hospital for the developmentally disabled, he moved into a house with some of the hospital residents. He saw the change in the persons he was living with. He saw how they gained confidence and became part of the local community. He started a similar home and then another. Today l'Arche communities can now be found throughout the world.

Jean Vanier is a quiet, unassuming man. He is able to form instant rapport both with handicapped persons and those who are not handicapped. In workshop people were divided into groups of handicapped and non-handicapped persons, encouraging them to discuss a variety topics and learn from each other and to recognize each person as an individual

On the last evening of Vanier's visit, the community celebrated a closing liturgy. One of the speakers who worked with the handicapped told us how much he learns each day from those he is supposed to be teaching. A developmentally disabled person told us how happy she was to have made so many good new friends. The last speaker was a person living in an l'Arche community who spoke of the miracles she had witnessed in her small home and the unbelievable changes in the people she lived with. She will always be a believer in the power of love.

When it came time for communion, all the priests in attendance were stationed at various places in the church, one distributed the wafers, two others passed out the wine. Father Bill, a friend if mine, had been with Vanier before so he was attuned to people with handicaps. The third person who approached his station for wine was a young Downes Syndrome woman. Father Bill said to her "Blood of Christ" then handed her the cup. Instead of just sipping the wine she drank it all. She handed the chalice back to Father Bill who looked at his empty cup and smiled. His job had been short lived. He went back to the altar with an empty cup but a beautiful memory.

Reverend Anderson, Sister Kraemer, Sister Jennings, Father Bill and Jean Vanier, have shown us that there is room for everyone in a faith community. Church, the one area of our society where total acceptance should be the standard, hasn't lived up to its potential. Individuals have, however, and through their efforts handicapped persons have been allowed to renew faith in all of us.

FATHER BOB

Father Bob Miller as a young priest. He is now retired, still a great friend and a great man.

In the early seventies Mimi and I purchased a home in a growing area of San Diego. The pastor Thomas Maloney of our parish church, a wonderful Irishman, scheduled masses to meet the needs of all his parishioners whether they be old church, new church or confused church. There was a no music mass, a choir mass, a hootenanny mass and a mixed mass that had a little bit of everything. Going to church became an adventure.

It was through our parish activities that we met Father Bob Miller, a priest of the new church. He was in his twenties. He seldom wore priestly garb, his hair was long, he drank beer, ate most of his meals at Jack in the Box and wore clothes that didn't always fit. He loved his church, the people and the changes that were bringing new life and challenge to that church. He was a priest for the times, a "hippie priest."

Father Bob became a part of our family and as part of our family; Father Bob became a part of Carlton's life too. Father Bob went with us on Saturday mornings when we had activities for Carlton and his friends living at Hilldale. Father Bob went along when we took the residents on trips to the circus or the movies. When Carlton came home for a visit Father Bob joined us for lunch or dinner.

It was obvious that there were no activities going on at Hilldale except the ones that we arranged on Saturday mornings. Nothing was offered to enrich the lives of the residents socially, mentally, physically or spiritually. No resident went to a church service and no ministers came to Hilldale. Yet, when we included hymns in our sing alongs, we noticed that many of the residents would join in. Since they knew these hymns, we decided we should give them a ritual that included their hymns. Father Bob volunteered to offer a mass at Hilldale.

Knowing the residents would respond to symbolism and music we planned a service that would be meaningful to them with candles, water, bells, colorful vestments and music as well as the bread and wine. We also prepared a slide show with slides of all the residents as part of the liturgy.

The day finally arrived for our Catholic service at Hilldale. Father Bob arrived in his priestly garb, black suit and Roman collar. One of the older residents, Faye, saw him and immediately genuflected and made the sign of the cross. Faye, in her early fifties, had been institutionalized since she was seven years old. Later she did a Mexican Hat Dance, revealing what a fun loving little girl she must have been. In 1973, when we did the liturgy, she had no living relatives. We'll never know the stories she and so many others who had been in institutions for over twenty years have had tell.

The mass was in the dining room. The altar was a table. The screen for the slide show was off to the side where everyone in the room could see it. There was a picture of Jesus behind the altar. Candles, flowers and a Crucifix were on the altar. Father Bob put on his multicolored vestment and the mass was ready to begin.

Musicians played guitars, banjos and tambourines and sang out a joyful tune as Father Bob proceeded down the center aisle, The congregation looked startled at the sight of such an impressive person dressed in the colors of the rainbow marching toward a table of flowers and pretty objects.

Some laughed, some waved hello and some clapped and yelled out greetings while others stared blankly into space.

Father Bob stood at the altar and pulled out a match. The flame from the match ignited the candles into two radiant halos. The worshippers were amazed at this bit of magic. Many watched this miracle in silence. Some, however, had to be restrained from running up to touch the flame. Others clapped, shouted and made appreciative noises. Few if any of them had ever seen a candle burning. Father Bob had really captured their attention.

Our hymns included, "Row, Row, Row Your Boat", "Happy Birthday to you", "Mary Had a Little Lamb" and "Michael Row Your Boat Ashore" so the people of God could join in the singing. All Father Bob said in his homily was "Jesus loves you." Some of the residents replied "I love Jesus." Like Faye, somewhere along the way they too must have had a religious experience.

Some of the more able residents brought the bread and wine to the altar for the communion service, very excited at having such an important role. As they advanced with great reverence up the center aisle, they were followed by Boris, a resident who had an aversion to wearing clothes. Reverently the gifts were handed to Father Bob by each of the gift bearers who then returned to his or her seat. Finally the only person in front of Father Bob was Boris, bare assed naked. Father Bob looked at him with an expression of holiness, wonder and awe and thanked him and the others as well for sharing all his gifts and returned to the altar. Boris was taken back to his room, redressed securely and returned to the service.

Father Bob blessed the bread and wine and said to everyone that Christ was truly with us. He raised the bread and the cup and prayed that the Lord's blessing would come to those who were assembled. A strange stillness filled the room. Everyone seemed to be caught up in the mystery of Christ being with us at that particular moment. Father Bob ate the bread and drank the wine and then distributed pieces of the bread to the gathered crowd. The bits of bread were eaten with zest. The noise level rose. For some reason only God knows, all the residents were focused in the same direction. For a brief time they seemed to have no handicaps.

After communion Father Bob again told them that Jesus loved each one of them. The musicians began playing "He's got the Whole World in

His Hands" and the slide show began. As each person's picture appeared on the large screen, we'd sing "He's got you and me John or Carlton or Faye in His hands." Some of the residents yelled at seeing themselves, some cried. Some jumped up and down. Others didn't seem to recognize themselves. We closed our mass with "Mary Had a Little Lamb." The singing was exuberant,. It had been a good day.

The "Streaker Mass" remains high on our list of fond memories. Sometimes when Mass seems routine and unexciting, my mind goes back to that special mass at Hilldale, the candles, the music, the flowers, the slide show and Boris bringing up his gifts in the all together. It was one day when I truly saw the face of Christ in every face of everyone there.

DEATH AND DYING

Mimi at Hilldale with Carlton and a couple of other residents. This is toward the end of Carlton's life. Carlton was always happy and he always made us happy.

When a resident of Hilldale dies, all the parents there lose a child. The loss is ours because all too often we're the only ones, beside the staff, who are aware of the person. If the resident has a family, we know the family. If there is no family, we're it. Death at Hilldale is a lonely event. Often it passes unnoticed.

Years ago when Carlton was first placed at Hilldale, the parents were dealt with individually. If something happened to our child their parents were the only ones who knew about it. If a resident passed away nothing was said. I found out about it in round about ways. Mrs. Mumford would say, "We have an empty bed" or "I'd like you to meet our new resident." She never came right out and said "Marcus died." She didn't want us to be upset.

I told Mrs. Mumford that the parents and staff needed to share the death of a resident; still it was sometimes weeks before we became aware of someone's death. Death is doubly upsetting if you find out about it long after the fact. Without mourning there is no closure

Today when a resident dies, a memorial service is arranged at Hilldale It is a time for parents, family, friends and staff to pay their final respects and say goodbye to a special part of their lives. Death is made a reality. We remember the person with stories about him or her. We recall incidents they were famous for during their stay at Hilldale. Once in awhile a death at Hilldale might make the death notices in the local newspaper but it will never make the obituaries. What do you write about a resident of Hilldale?

Marcus was the Christ Child in our Christmas Pageant. He was a Thalidomide baby, born with no arms or legs. If that wasn't handicap enough, he was also retarded and black. Marcus wasn't helpless, however. He learned to use the body God had given him to scoot around. It was amazing how fast he could get around the facility. Staff found him in the dining room, another resident's room, the nursing station or even out side if the door had been left open. He loved being picked up and cuddled. He touched the heart of everyone he ever met.

There was no memorial service for Marcus. They didn't tell us he caught pneumonia and died. I found out by chance weeks later when I asked one of the aides why I hadn't seen Marcus around.

The same thing happened to Mary, a lively and well liked teenager. She greeted everyone who came into Hilldale. When we went on field trips, the volunteers loved to get Mary as their partner. She was always fun. One day Mary wasn't there to greet me when I came to visit. I realized I hadn't seen Mary for quite some time. When I asked about her, I was told she had died earlier that month. Later I found out Mary had choked on a peanut butter and jelly sandwich. Mrs. Mumford said," I didn't tell you because I didn't want you to be upset,"

At the time if there was no immediate family involved, Hilldale didn't bother to tell us that someone living there had passed away. Maybe they felt we would have been upset with them because someone in their care had died. Maybe they were upset with themselves for being helpless for having lost someone.

When Michelle died she was one of the residents you wouldn't recognize if you didn't work with her. She wasn't a greeter. You had to seek her out. When you found her, her eyes would sparkle. Michelle made you feel important. I found out she had died when I was introduced to a new resident three weeks after her death. Michelle was a quiet woman. When I told the other parents that her heart had finally given out, they asked to see a photograph of her. They didn't recognize Michelle by name.

Marcus, Mary and Michelle had no relatives who were involved with them. When they died, no arrangements were made for funerals or memorial services. Sad to say they were taken from Hilldale and given a paupers grave. There was no fanfare, no ceremony, no good-byes, there was, only an empty bed soon to be filled by a new client.

Some who died we knew about because we knew their parents. Others like Faye we knew because she made it a point to be known. She was the oldest and friendliest person living at Hilldale. She was the woman who genuflected when Father Bob came into the facility. She was the one who did the Mexican Hat Dance. Faye was placed in a mental hospital over fifty years ago. She had no past history and no living relatives. If only she could have talked, what a story she would have told.

We had a memorial service for Faye. Nancy Seppala, our social worker wrote a prayer for Faye's memorial:

Dear Lord,

> *You have a soul that came to you recently who is known to you as Faye Wrubliska. Today we are gathered here to say our good-byes and to celebrate her freedom, for only in our souls are we truly free.*
>
> *Faye's journey in life was not an easy one, for she was mentally retarded. A large part of her life was spent in a system that treated the mentally retarded as second class citizens. Maybe the system didn't always care, but I'll bet that all those that cared and worked with Faye through the many years did, and remember her still in their hearts. She was a special lady, an individual human being not a label of retarded, but a woman with pride and dignity to the very end.*
>
> *Lord, help us to continue to grow in our consciousness, to continue to understand and be sensitive to those reaching out to us and depending on*

us. Give us strength to meet the challenge of this life and in the end, as Faye did, meet death with pride and dignity.

Faye too was given a pauper's grave.

Vernon, Everett and Theresa's parents were active in our parent group. Vernon had a funeral mass at his Catholic parish in San Diego. Many people came to celebrate his sheltered life. It enabled us to share our grief. Vernon's death was made easier for the family to accept because we were there for them, they were not left alone.

When Theresa died, I was able to arrange a memorial service for her. In the tribute I read at her service, I said, "Sometimes we wonder about Theresa's life. A life like hers or anyone who is severely handicapped can be very purposeful just as any life can. We're all here to find joy and bring that joy to others. If we accomplish these two things then we have accomplished a lot in the time that has been allotted to us on this earth. Theresa in her short lifetime brought love and joy to many."

Everett's family lived in San Diego and wanted a memorial at Hilldale, Everett's home. Their minister came and we talked about Everett and the memories we had of him. At his memorial service I did not have memories to share. Everett and I exchanged 'hellos' in the halls of Hilldale for years and that was the extent of our interaction. In all those years I didn't know him because he was just always there saying 'hello.' The staff that worked with him every day knew him and talked of how he had a wonderful personality. They told stories of the funny things Everett did. I learned a lot about Everett at his memorial service. What a shame that throughout all those years, I hardly knew him because I never took the time to say anything other than 'hello' to him.

Memorial services are now a regular occurrence when a resident dies and die they do. Their main families are the workers at Hilldale. It might not be the same as losing a family member but it hurts just the same. The memorial services not only bring closure to the life of a real person but meaning to the people who have made that life worth living. No matter the burial place of a person living or dying at Hilldale at least now they go with a sense of joy and dignity.

DARUISH

A Valentine form Carlton. He was in his 30's in this picture

Mrs. Mumford retired from Hilldale after serving more than thirty years. She was the only administrator Mimi and I had dealt with since Carlton was placed there. After years of struggle the parents and Mrs. Mumford had finally reached an understanding. Parents were able to express their concerns. We also learned to listen to her explanations. We knew she genuinely loved the residents and the staff at Hilldale.

We were uneasy with her leaving, yet welcomed change. Hilldale needed new leadership, new ideas and a new spirit. Still we feared the unknown. Would a new administrator listen to our concerns or know our children? Would new ownership be able to operate Hilldale in its present condition? Would Hilldale be closed? All we knew was that Care Incorporated, the present owner, was in bankruptcy.

As Mrs. Mumford was cleaning out her desk, we reminisced about all the things that had happened over the years. Eighteen years we had worked together. Some of those years we would have liked to forget while others stood out as years of real change and progress and a better life for every resident of Hilldale.

While I was there she introduced me to her replacement, Mr. Washington. Mr. Washington told me the new owners were going to clean up Hilldale and make it parent friendly. He gave me his home phone number and assured me that he would be available to the parents day and night. At our parent meeting he told of the positive changes that were going to take place to the physical plant and to the staffing of Hilldale. He looked forward to our input. We hadn't heard anyone ask for our input in eighteen years and didn't know quite what to think.

Mr. Washington made changes right and left. He got rid of all the good consultants and many of the long term staff. When I asked him why he was letting all the key people go, he said he wanted his own people working with him. The staff he let go knew the residents and they knew the programs. The ones he hired knew nothing. He seemed to be making changes for the sake of change.

His administration ended within six weeks. He had no license. Care Incorporated was still operating Hilldale but at reduced costs.

I discovered Mr. Washington was gone when I arrived at Hilldale one day and was greeted by a new administrator, Rodney. Rodney said Care Incorporated had placed him at Hilldale to undo what Washington had done. He told me that Hilldale would be out of escrow soon. He hoped to stay on with the new owners.

Rodney told me the new owners were going to make a lot of positive changes to the physical plant and to the staffing of Hilldale. I told Rodney the parents had heard that before and were concerned about the way some excellent staff had been lost the last time those words were uttered. He said he was already calling staff members and offering their jobs back.

Rodney had been with Care Incorporated for many years. He had been the administrator at Bloomington Convalescent, Carlton's first placement, twenty-three years before. He made himself available to the parents. He listened to our concerns. He seemed to be someone the parents could work with.

Just before Rodney arrived, the parents had purchased equipment for the back yard. We were in the process of having it put in place when Hilldale went into escrow. We spent nine thousand dollars on the equipment and labor. Care Incorporated had agreed to finish the project by replacing the worn out shade net. When I asked Rodney if there was any hope for a new shade net, he said it was in the budget and part of the escrow so not to worry. The netting never came through.

Two months after Rodney arrived, Hilldale was still in escrow. He kept saying we would meet the new owners soon. We wondered if there really were new owners. One day Rodney introduced me to Daruish and Malou Razavi and their three year old daughter. Daruish was in his early forties, Malou was a bit younger. I figured they were looking over Hilldale as a possible placement for a child.

I was taken by surprise when Rodney said, "These are the new owners." Convalescent facilities are owned by corporations. I asked him if he had bought Care Incorporated. He said, "No, we have only bought Hilldale."

Daruish told me of his plans to make Hilldale the best place for our son and all the other residents. I had my doubts. I couldn't believe anyone would buy a for profit facility that housed fifty-seven severely handicapped men and women, especially one that was in bankruptcy but it sure sounded good.

Daruish was a different kind of owner. He was a businessman who felt that Hilldale, properly run, could be both profitable and an excellent place for the residents. He was optimistic the day I met him and he's optimistic today.

At our first meeting he told me Rodney would remain in charge of the day to day operations. When escrow closed, he said he would be at Hilldale to get a feel for the residents and the facility. He had never been involved with severely handicapped people. This was his family's first experience with developmentally disabled of any kind. I couldn't believe what I was hearing.

Escrow closed and, true to his word, Daruish and Malou were at Hilldale every day. Over dinner one evening, we told Daruish our hopes and our frustrations. We reviewed mistakes of the past, staff turnover, distrust between parents and facility. We talked about the good people who worked at Hilldale. We told them what the parents had done in the past and what they could do to make Hilldale better. We all agreed that by working together we could make Hilldale the best facility of its kind in the West. When Mimi and I returned home that night, we were excited. After eighteen years something positive was happening at Hilldale. We felt hopeful, but we cautioned each other about getting our hopes too high. Time would tell if Daruish and Malou were for real or were just saying what we wanted to hear.

In the weeks that followed most of Daruish's efforts went into making repairs on the building and the grounds. Care Incorporated had left Hilldale in terrible shape. The roof leaked the parking area had to be resurfaced, the cement floor in the entry way had to be torn up so the fire sprinkler system could be replaced and the bathrooms had to be retiled. The new outdoor equipment the parents had purchased was still covered by the worn out shade screen.

When the repairs were completed Daruish began making long overdue improvements. He refurbished the nurses' station, painted the halls, carpeted the entrance hall, put sinks in the dining rooms, wallpapered the offices and meeting rooms, hung pictures and put new and larger shade screen over the recreation area. Hilldale was looking good.

Daruish was proud of his refurbishing. He hadn't been aware of all the disrepair that resulted from twenty years of neglect. He just kept on fixing what had to be fixed and improving what had to be improved. He showed me his books, the costs of staffing, feeding and maintaining Hilldale each month. He showed me his break even point. He saw Hilldale as potentially a successful business venture for him and his family. I hoped Daruish would own and operate Hilldale forever.

About two months after Daruish took over the ownership of Hilldale, I walked in the office and was greeted by a new administrator, Dr. George. He was a nice man, good with people, sincere. He was not a very competent administrator. He spent a lot of time on Hilldale's front porch smoking cigarettes but Hilldale needed to have a licensed administrator and Dr. George had a license.

Daruish told me he had to get rid of Rodney because he had a record of offenses that made him a risk as an administrator. Care Incorporated hadn't bothered to tell Daruish about Rodney's problems when they made him interim administrator. It seems Care Incorporated neglected to tell Daruish a lot of the problems he would inherit with Hilldale.

Daruish managed to replace several people who were well intentioned but non productive. Staff training was intensified. If demands were more than a staff member felt he or she could handle, the staff member was free to leave. Care and programming was improved a hundredfold.

Daruish worked to bring Hilldale up to code and meet all the licensing requirements for a facility of its kind. He worked with all the agencies involved. He asked Regional Center to help him when programs that look good on paper were impossible to put into practice. He worked with the State when questionable demands were made of Hilldale. In the past each agency had its own agenda, unaware of what other agencies demanded. By getting the agencies to work together, Daruish overcame many barriers. Working together worked wonders. Everyone involved with Hilldale was feeling extremely positive until Licensing came in for a week of review for the certification of Hilldale

When Care Incorporated owned Hillsdale, a visit by Licensing caused instant paranoia. Everyone from the top down lived in terror of the Licensing team. The team found nothing but fault with Hilldale. The administration started preparing for Licensing about six weeks before they were due to arrive. Staff was upgraded. Records were brought up to the minute. Programs were properly followed and logged into the resident's logbook. Maintenance, long put off, was brought up to standard. By the time Licensing arrived, everyone at Hilldale was emotionally drained.

During this time Daruish was studying to get his administrators license as the administrators he was hiring proved to be inept. He got rid of Dr. George and asked Mrs. Mumford to fill in until he had his own license.

Before Daruish took over Hilldale when Licensing made its yearly visit to assess Hilldale, the whole facility became paranoid. Licensing would check every aspect of Hilldale's operation. To prepare for the annual visit, more staff would be hired, staff would work overtime memorizing the needs of each resident in case Licensing would question them. The place was cleaned up and made to smell good. The inspectors from Licensing were at the facility from early morning to late at night for one whole week. At the end of the week, they had a debriefing with the administrative staff and reviewed all the violations they had found. Soon the written report arrived with its many citations and paranoia turned to gloom. For the next eleven months everyone worked on improving the areas. Then it was time for the process to begin again. Licensing paranoia was cyclical. It seemed the cycle could never be broken.

The first time Licensing came to assess Hilldale during Daruish's ownership, Daruish was sure things would be different. He worked with all government agencies. His staff was well trained. The physical plant had been improved. As far as he was concerned, Licensing could have come in anytime.

In spite of his efforts, when Licensing came for Hilldale's annual review, the team found nothing good. They cited the kitchen, programs, lack of knowledge on the part of the aides, poor records, broken furniture and all kinds of trivial discrepancies. They gave Daruish and his staff no encouragement. Nothing was said about all the improvements he had made. They even hinted that if he didn't correct things quickly, they would suggest reprimands, fines or even closure. Daruish was devastated. The staff was in shock.

At our request, our Social Worker arranged a meeting of four parents including Mimi and me, with the three women who were involved in the Licensing review. We told them of our concerns about fines and possible closure. They assured us that Hilldale would not close, that Hilldale wasn't really all that bad. I told them that the owner and his staff didn't seem to be getting that message. One of the women said they mentioned fines and closure to hurry along the needed upgrading.

We defended Hilldale and Daruish. We told them of all the improvements that had taken place during the past year. We explained that threatening Hilldale was threatening our kids. I mentioned that this same harsh criticism happened every time Licensing came through. There were years we could have understood closing Hilldale but this was not one of them. We asked them why they had never invited the input of parents to gauge what happened year in and year out. They told us it had never seemed necessary. We asked if they ever looked at improvements. One of the women looked at us and said," Our job is to only look for things that are bad." After the meeting one of the other parents said to me, "How'd you like to have a job like that- only looking for things that are bad?!"

Daruish was ready to throw in the towel. He felt he had done more than enough at Hilldale to be credited with moving in the right direction. No! Licensing could only see things that were wrong. At the final meeting Daruish said he was more than willing to close Hilldale down if it was as bad as they said it was. The woman in charge of the review quickly assured Daruish that there would be no fines or closure, that the citations were merely areas he should focus on to make Hilldale even better. Then she congratulated him for having such a supportive group of parents.

Daruish was relieved but angry. Before he became the owner of Hilldale this same group from Licensing had reviewed Hilldale for certification. Although few of the deficiencies had ever been corrected by the former ownership when it was a large corporation, Licensing had done nothing about it. Now, when an individual took over the operation, they dumped on him. He was justifiably angry.

Daruish took the list of citations and corrected each one. The equipment that was cited was upgraded and areas of weakness were pointed out to the staff so they could perform their jobs more efficiently. He purchased new equipment for programs, new mattresses and new materials for activities.

Bussing the residents to their programs and back became a serious problem for Hilldale and Daruish. Because the bus company was contracted by Regional Center, they felt they had no responsibility to Hilldale except to transport residents. Hilldale had to abide by the bus company's schedules, no matter how inconvenient. The residents had to get up at five A.M., get dressed, eat and be ready to catch their bus as early as six-thirty.

The buses had no chair lifts so the persons in wheel chairs were pushed up a ramp. Pushing the wheel chairs up and down that ramp caused wear and tear and frequently put the wheelchairs out of commission. Bussing was costing Hilldale time and money. If Daruish complained, the Bus Company and Regional Center would make excuses. They made it appear as much Hilldale's fault as the bus company's. One afternoon one of the residents dropped four feet in his wheel chair when the bus driver forgot the ramp. Daruish gave up and bought his own buses.

Once Hilldale had its own buses, hours for Carlton and his friends became more normal. They were able to sleep later and go to bed later. The buses had lifts for the wheel chairs. The wheel chairs stopped breaking down. The bus drivers were hired by Daruish. The aides on the buses worked at Hilldale so they knew the persons who were riding the bus. On weekends the residents could go out. It was a major improvement for Hilldale.

Regional Center pays for transporting the handicapped to and from their programs. When Daruish started transporting the residents on his own buses, he was informed that he would get less per trip than the bus company. When he questioned the policy, he was told that the bus company had more buses and more overhead so they had to have a special contract. That special contract paid the bus company almost double what Hilldale was paid for transportation.

Hilldale was transporting its residents all over the county to their programs. It made no sense to Daruish so he began his own program closer to Hilldale. The Advantage Center became a showplace for how creative programs could benefit severely handicapped individuals.

When a resident left Hilldale for a less restricted living situation, they often failed and were retuned to Hilldale if there was an opening. If not they were placed somewhere else. This bothered Daruish so he opened two group homes for the residents that were ready to leave Hilldale.

When Daruish took ownership of Hilldale, he told me he wanted Hilldale to be the best facility of its kind in the West. I had wanted the same thing for eighteen years. I encouraged him, but I had my doubts that he'd ever do it. As I look back, I realize I saw it happen. Parents and Daruish worked together and made the bedrooms more homelike for the residents. The back yard was upgraded. Transportation was made available, the Advantage Center was established and now group homes are available. Licensing can come in any time, Hilldale is a welcoming place. Being the best facility of its kind in the West is no longer a dream, it's a reality.

When the parents put on their annual Appreciation Dinner to honor staff members who have been at Hilldale for five years or more, we included Daruish and Malou and some of the new people because only one person had worked at Hilldale for over five years. It was a special evening, an evening that the parents and Hilldale finally came together as a team.

Carlton continued to live at Hilldale, the best facility of its kind in the West, for ten more years.

FINAL DAYS

Baby Carlton and his Uncle Jerry. Two great guys who are no longer here physically but in our hearts

Carlton passed away in June of 1999. He'd lived to be forty years old. He might have lived longer, but his stay at Pacific State Hospital when he was eight years old exposed him to hepatitis, from that time on Carlton had problems with his liver. It finally caught up with him during the last few years of his life. He was in and out of the hospital during that time. He fought it to the end.

Mimi and I knew his time was limited when he went to the hospital in early May. He looked so sick and tired that we prayed for the Good Lord to take him gently through his remaining days. We spent a lot of time at the hospital holding his hand and comforting him. While he was there we spent a lot of time dealing with a hospital staff that we felt tried hard but was ignorant of a patient like Carlton. Our suspicions were aroused when a speech therapist told us she had had a talk with Carlton. Knowing Carlton had never said a word in his life, we were concerned. Then the nutritionist told us Carlton was spitting up and fearing that he might choke they decided to put him on a totally liquid diet. We tried to explain that Carlton had been spitting up since he was two years old and please, give him some food as he does love to eat. They held their ground so we had to sneak in yogurt and the food he liked so he wouldn't starve. Psychiatrist and psychologist came in to work on his behavior. Even a dentist showed up to repair his teeth. Doctors and nurses were concerned about his progress. They asked us all kinds of questions that we couldn't answer. We referred them to Hilldale where all his medical records and medications were carefully recorded every day. The staff from Hilldale came often to take Carlton on walks and keep up some kind of routine that he was accustomed to. They even snuck in some food as they too were worried about his insatiable appetite.

After a few days the social worker arranged a discharge conference. Mimi and I and the head nurse from Hilldale were there as were the nutritionist, psychologist, speech therapist and the hospital staff. After much discussion Mimi and I and the Hilldale nurse convinced them that Carlton would be much better off returning to Hilldale. The people at the meeting disagreed but let the parents rule the day.

Carlton did not return to Hilldale cured, but he did return happy. He seemed to improve during the following weeks so Mimi and I and my brother Jerry and his wife Aljeanne took advantage of an invitation to spend a week house sitting for their son and his wife in their home at Moss Beach. Their home had a fantastic view of the Pacific Ocean. It was the perfect place for the four of us to escape the rigors of San Diego. We bought our supplies and settled in for a much appreciated week of relaxation. The first night we went out to celebrate my birthday at The Moss Beach Distillery; a gourmet restaurant nestled in the hills overlooking the ocean. Our vacation was off to a great start.

When we got home that night, there was a message to call our daughter Alicia in San Diego. We called and Alicia told us Carlton had been taken to the hospital soon after we left. He was terminal so she had insisted he be taken to the San Diego Hospice. They argued against such a placement but she insisted and said that Carlton as well and Mimi and I deserved it. "Look at him." She told the doctor. At this point Carlton was completely bald from alopecia, frail from being sick and had a Buddha belly because of liver problems. "I know he might not look like much but this guy has changed the lives of many. If he has to go let's have him go out in style. Plus my parents don't need to see him in some sad place. They have seen enough of that!" The doctors questioned WHO had the authority to make this decision? Alicia did what the entire family had been doing for forty years…whatever it took. "Well, Me." She smiled "I have the power of attorney." She was thankful at this point that Carlton had never learned to talk because she was convinced he would have called her out for lying like any big brother would. They placed him at Hospice. That was where he was at that moment and Alicia was sleeping there that night. So much for our vacation.

After speaking with Carlton's doctor we decided to spend the night at Moss Beach and head back to San Diego first thing in the morning. That night my brother had a bad bout of food poisoning from some pork he had eaten at a Mexican restaurant on our trip to Moss Beach. I didn't know if we should go to a hospital in the area or bee line it to San Diego. Jerry insisted he was fine and we should get on the road, so we set out for San Diego. We were thinking of Carlton, hoping he would be alive when we got to San Diego. At the same time we were watching and hoping, my brother too, would be alive at journey's end.

We arrived home about six that evening. We got my brother into bed and headed for the San Diego Hospice hoping and praying that Carlton was still hanging on. When we found his room he was still alive and seemed relieved to hear our voices. Alicia, her husband Bill and her son Patrick were there and so was our daughter Colleen with her little boy, Max. Carlton had just had his fill of various desserts. When Colleen arrived they had delivered Carlton a tray with dinner. Colleen looked at Alicia and said "Look, we need to feed him dessert first in case it is the last thing he ever eats." The sisters agreed this was the only plan that made any sense and the kind staff at hospice brought in a variety of treats. Carlton, true to form until the last ate every bite.

The San Diego Hospice is a beautiful facility overlooking Mission Valley. The landscaping is conducive to peace and tranquility with beautiful trees, flowers and park like grass areas. The people working there are wonderful. They know the stress the families feel and gently help them through this trying time. There are many volunteers who are there to assist you and make you comfortable at this stressful time. The atmosphere at hospice is one of tranquility rather than tension and fear.

We were exhausted after our long drive so after an hour or two we went home. Alicia and Patrick had gone home earlier. Colleen and Max wanted to stay with Carlton and were able to have beds right in his room. Sleep that night did not come easy. We returned early the next morning to be with our son and comfort him on his journey. To cheer him up we brought him his favorite toy, a stuffed duck that quacked when you squeezed it. Its quack sounded just like Carlton. That afternoon our son Tom showed up from San Luis Obispo. Carlton responded when he saw and heard his brother. It was as though all would be well as the whole family was together again. It was a good day as we shared many memories of this silent son and brother that had meant so much. We shared the times he hid from us or stole our food, his double jointedness, his Christmas plays, his doctor visits, our trip to New York, the times he came home and the times we spent at Hilldale. Memories were flooding our minds while we were with him at hospice.

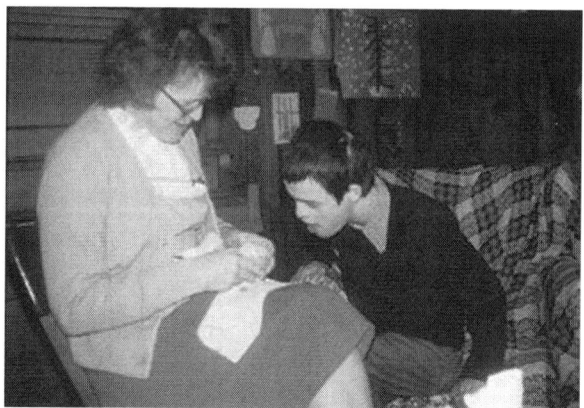

Carlton and his mother.....they shared a love of oranges!

Colleen spent another night at hospice while Mimi, Tom and I went home to get some rest. The third day Mimi spent some time alone with her son while I was running errands. While she was there a volunteer came in to give Carlton a massage. She looked at Carlton and then at Mimi and told Mimi she needed the massage more than Carlton and proceeded to give her a much needed working over. When I came back, I found my wife looking more relaxed than I'd seen her in weeks. The nurse explained to us what it would be like during Carlton's last moments. She told us his dying would be much more difficult for us than it would be for him. Mimi wanted to spend the night with her son. I went home and planned to be back about ten the next morning, spend the day and stay there that night.

The next morning the phone rang about quarter to nine. It was Mimi. She was crying she told me Carlton had passed away minutes ago. His time hadn't come early that morning so the nurse insisted that Mimi go to breakfast. Mimi told Carlton she'd be right back so he mustn't leave. The nurse reassured her that she would stay with Carlton so he would not be alone. Mimi went to the cafeteria and had a bite to eat. When she retuned to be with Carlton, he began to fail just as the nurse had said. Within a matter of minutes Carlton died with his mother at his side holding his hand.

Carlton and Mimi. He always greeted her with his sweet smile

Our family got to hospice to see Carlton for the last time soon after he died. It was a trying time to say goodbye to a son and brother. As we were leaving, each one with their own thoughts, Carlton's stuffed duck quacked. We all looked at one another and laughed. Carlton got in the last word.

A few days after Carlton died we arranged for two memorial services. One was at our church, the other at Hilldale. The word of Carlton's death got around. About two hundred people showed up at our church on the night of the memorial service. They were there to bid Carlton farewell and comfort our family for the loss of our son and their brother. Our pastor gave a beautiful tribute to Carlton. He didn't know him personally, but he did know him through conversations with Mimi and me over the years. Through his ministry he had come in contact with many families with developmentally disabled members and was able to speak of the positive impact they had on their families and those around them. I gave the eulogy for Carlton and his sounds of silence.

> One of the big hits of the 60s was Simon and Garfunkel's, "The Sounds of Silence". It's a beautiful concept, the sounds of silence. When I hear that song, I think about gentleness and my son Carlton. Carlton has made himself silently known for over forty years. He makes noises but he speaks no words-never has. Carlton's mother and I try to understand his noises, but we can only guess at what they mean. There's a strawberry sound, a happy sound, an "I'm not going to do whatever it is," sound, an "I'm feeling good," sound, and an "I feel crummy," sound.
>
> The strawberry sound, "um um um umm," sound, comes during strawberry season. Carlton uses it when he is presented with strawberries and whipped cream. When I hear "um um um umm" my own mouth begins to water.
>
> If Carlton decides he doesn't want to do something, we hear "naa naa naa na!" He makes it very clear that he doesn't plan to do whatever it is that he's naa na-ing about. He has "naa naaed" about getting into a car, going to bed, sitting in a chair, getting a haircut or having a TV channel changed. He doesn't go into a lot of detail but we understand. When Carlton's in high spirits he more or less quacks, which sounds something like "quack quack quack" It's one of his loudest sounds. When we go to Hilldale, the facility where Carlton lives, and hear him quacking three rooms away, we feel good because we know Carlton's feeling good. What a simple way to express joy!
>
> Carlton also has a laughing sound. It's a mischievous "ah ah ah ah" sound which seems to say" I know what your thinking, but you're probably

wrong". Carlton's "ah ahs' are playful and full of happiness. Ah ahs" are contagious. You respond to "ah ahs" with hugs and affection. "If 'ah ahs" touch enough people the world is bound to change. They're Carlton's special gift to the world.

When Carlton's not feeling well, he lets out a steady moaning sound "unh unh unh unhunh." Any one can tell he's not feeling too good. Many years ago we were very frightened when Carlton made his "unh unh unh" sound. He couldn't tell us what was wrong so we took him to the hospital. Dr. Harris knew by the "unh unh unhs" that Carlton was hurting. When he finally got around to examining Carlton's ear for infection, Carlton began to quack. Carlton had told us where the problem was. He was happy because Dr. Harris had found the hurt. A little medicine, a little love and Carlton was back to his old "quack quack, naa naa, um um, ah ah" self.

Carlton has one other sound that drives us up the wall. He grinds his teeth. It certainly gets him plenty of attention. Maybe that's why he does it. We know it has nothing to do with strawberries, not doing something, feeling good, feeling bad or laughing. Maybe it's the sound that gives him the feeling that we get from reading a good book or hearing a great song. Maybe he doesn't even hear the grinding sound. For Carlton it's the sound of silence.

Yes, Carlton in his quiet way says many things to many people. He makes us understand where he's at without a word, just a few sounds. Mimi and I, on the other hand, talk for hours, using a vast number of words and yet neither one of us understands the other. We don't know what made Carlton the way he was, quiet and almost silent, but when he was around, there was a feeling of gentleness that comes from his "sound of silence."

It was a wonderful send off for Carlton. Those who were there left knowing Carlton a little better than when they arrived.

The following night we celebrated his life at Hilldale with the parents of the residents and the staff. The owners, Dariush and his family put out a feast for all those who were there. Father Bob was the celebrant for the evening. He knew Carlton and spoke of his encounters with him. He then asked those who were there to share their thoughts on Carlton and their own experiences raising a severely handicapped child or working with Developmentally Disabled people. The sharing was extraordinary. The love of the parents for their children, the difficulties of raising their handicapped child the awesome task of placing their child in the care of others brought home the way people cope with situations that are presented to them out of the blue. The concern the workers shared for the parents and the folks they were entrusted with was beautiful to hear. Father Bob was moved to tears from the love that was at Hilldale that evening. He often told me how he integrated those sharings into his homilies over the years. I read about Carlton's sounds of silence and then each person there was given a balloon as a symbol of our rising to heaven on our final journey. We let our balloons go.

Upwards they went in a mass of color. One lonely balloon never got off the ground. Bob looked at me and said, "Carlton just wasn't ready to go yet". It had been a very moving evening.

Seven months after Carlton's death, tragedy again struck our family. Little Max, our grandson had accidentally drowned in San Francisco. Losing such a beautiful young child is difficult to comprehend. Father Bob was there to be with our family and comfort our daughter Colleen. At Max's memorial service in a packed church Father Bob and Colleen put together a beautiful tribute to Little Max. At the end of Max's memorial we were all given balloons. We walked up a hill to a little garden Colleen had planted in Max's memory. Bob spoke of the significance of the balloons. He told us to let them go. Colleen's balloon, Mimi's balloon and my balloon led the colorful flight. This time every balloon sailed heavenward, Father Bob turned to me and said," Carlton decided that now was the time for him to leave and be with his young nephew, Max".

A few weeks later Father Bob sent us a letter he said he received from Carlton:

> My dear family,
>
> My name is Carlton. I am a very special miracle of God. God loves me and I love God. God, you know, has been good to me. He has given me a loving family, my sisters Colleen and Alicia and my brother Tom, who are

very special to me. God's love came to me in a very special way through my mother and father, who were His gift to me. It was through them that I came to experience unconditional love and acceptance. It was in my mother's womb, that I first found God's presence, in her joy and excitement of birthing me. Yes, I have a good family, who were given to me for special reasons that God himself — and now I also — know.

Why God chose me to be Carlton, I now know. You will not know this until we meet again in the Kingdom that has been promised to us by Jesus, my brother and yours. God gave me a special gift: He sent me for love; to bring people closer together. He gave me the gift of a free spirit to touch others in my own friendly and humorous way so that in me, Carlton, they could see God's love at work. He chose me to be me so that when you helped and cared for me you could touch God himself and so that in your love for me I could know God.

I, Carlton, want you all to be at peace with yourselves as I am with myself and with God, as I am at peace with Jesus, who gave himself for me, as I am at peace with the Holy Spirit who gives us all the peace of mind and the peace of heart that we seek. This evening I want to assure you all that I will try to be that instrument of peace and love for all of you.

My name is Carlton and now I am a saint. I have a special place in God's Kingdom. I never dreamed this could happen to me. But it has. One day, it will happen to you too. I am waiting for you to join me in the Resurrection that I have experienced and I will welcome you with great JOY. In the meantime, let God's love live in your hearts by trusting him, loving each other, and caring for those in need. Until we meet again my prayers will be with you each day.

I love you
I love you.

WHAT WILL BE WILL BE

Mimi and I today

When I started writing about Special Love it centered on Carlton. Carlton brought our whole family together in a special way. Colleen, Tom and Alicia always asked about his well being when they phoned. His aunts and uncles had him in their thoughts. When his brother and sisters were in town they visited Hilldale. Developmentally Disabled people are a part of their lives. They know what it's like having a severely handicapped brother. It is no big deal, they grew from it.

There's always something new happening in the treatment of Developmentally Disabled persons. Some new ideas are old ideas with new names. Some new techniques are only fads and are soon forgotten. One thing certain is that there are a lot of severely handicapped people to deal with. They come in all ages and they come with new disabilities and handicaps. There are crack babies, babies born with AIDS, children disabled because of abuse, physical and sexual. Severely handicapped children grow to adulthood and old age. Each day new programs develop to help them become more self sufficient. It's a real problem for society but it's one that can be managed in ways beneficial to all.

The disability climate has changed so much over the years that Carlton and children like him with Downes Syndrome have become the easiest to manage. They are diagnosed at birth or in many cases even before they are born. While they are still infants, the parents receive help. They enter infant programs and often go to regular kindergarten classes. After kindergarten, many are mainstreamed into regular school programs. The lower functioning still attend special programs. These programs are on public school sites. Children with handicaps are no longer isolated in their own special schools, sheltered from their sisters and brothers.

As children with disabilities grow older they are trained on job sites so they, like the rest of us, can take pride and be rewarded for a job well done. Some work at McDonalds, others in the clothing industry, still others work as gardeners and maids. That's a big change from when Carlton was born. We were told to place him in a state hospital right away. It would save us the grief of raising a hopeless child.

Over the years persons with Downes Syndrome have taught us a lot. They've shown us by their actions that there is no limit to what they can accomplish. Movies and television have given us a peek at the possibilities. They can read, ride bicycles, swim and act. They can operate in the workplace and live alone. Last Sunday, I even saw an ad for Downes Syndrome dolls.

Who knows what genetic development might take place in the years to come. Nothing surprises me. In 1959 they discovered that all Downes Syndrome persons have an extra chromosome. Someday maybe they'll be able to do something genetically about it before a Downes Syndrome child is born.

Sad to say some professionals had higher expectations for Carlton and the residents of Hilldale than their parents did. We raised our children when the most that was expected of them was to eat and sleep. We didn't even believe they could be potty trained. The philosophy now is that everyone has the ability to do something. The task is to develop the skills of each individual to the point where he or she, no matter the disability, can function in some way. It was difficult for Mimi and me to see the possibility of Carlton developing skills of any kind. It was also hard for us to support programs that developed those skills. We saw them as efforts in futility. No matter what we thought then, it's happening now.

There's a move on to make living arrangements for the handicapped more normal. It's being proposed that homes, housing no more than twelve handicapped persons, will serve all Developmentally Disabled persons no matter the severity of their handicap. This type housing would do away with all large facilities like Hilldale. Again the parents are having a hard time with this. Since Dariush has owned Hilldale the quality of care has improved dramatically. The parents are comfortable knowing that a nurse is on site twenty four hours a day. Even though the staff at Hilldale turns over frequently, the parents know the programs for their sons and daughters are being carried out with consistency. Even if Daruish and Malou decide to get out of the care provider business, I don't feel Hilldale will close. I've heard stories of group home operators quitting because of age or sickness. When that happens the scramble is on to find new housing. Often the new housing seems to be in other cities. Mimi and I knew a normal life style and living conditions were the ultimate hope for Carlton. We just didn't see it as necessary during his life.

Recently a state hospital has set up a group home for four of its residents on the hospital grounds. This seems a little different than dispersing Hilldale residents in group homes around San Diego. Daruish also has plans for a couple of small community homes. They will serve as halfway houses between Hilldale and community group homes. This seems more appropriate to me. If a resident can't make it in the community home, he or she could come back for more training at Hilldale. I've visited some homes and apartment living arrangements for the Developmentally Disabled. Some are excellent; some leave a lot to be desired. A lot depends on the help and who's running them.

Hilldale is still making improvements. Improvements that will help the residents increase their skills and improve their behavior. A room is being equipped with computers, audio equipment, switches and manipulative types of materials that will enable the residents to acquire new specific skills. These skills, learned over time, might prepare the residents for the changes that seem destined to take place.

Aging is another area of concern. When Carlton was born, his life expectancy was seven and a half years. The short life span was predicted because these children were placed in state hospitals shortly after birth. Care and hygiene were neglected in the state hospitals, disease followed and soon the children would die. Deinstitutionalization. changed that in late sixties. Now there would be no limit to how long Carlton would live. Some of the residents at Hilldale are in their sixties. They are becoming senior citizens. Like senior citizens everywhere, they will have special needs. Many senior citizens don't like to be around kids all the time. They will tell you they love their grand children, but not for more than a couple of days at a time. The same is true of the Developmentally Disabled. They too become impatient with younger folks around them. They need to be with people their own age. They need their own types of programs. They need to be secure.

Carlton, because he was Downes Syndrome, would have developed Alzheimer's disease. Medical studies have shown that all persons with Downes Syndrome will develop this terrible ailment when they get older. In his last year, we could see the tell tale signs on Carlton. It was beginning to restrict his ability to walk and he spent more time in bed.

Carlton came a long way for never having said a word. Human life is truly amazing. Carlton's life brought us special love in so many ways. Special Love through people like Gladys and Carlton's great aunt Dot, Mrs. Mumford and Daruish, Captain Sticky, Father Bob, Santa Claus and the parents at Hilldale. We've found Special Love at his schools, in church, Regional Center, Hospitals and doctors offices. We've found Special Love in our family and friends, on holidays, at Christmas parties and Pageants. We've witnessed Special Love in the persons living at Hilldale.

Mimi wrote a letter for our church paper a few years back. It concerned Carlton and the celebration of life;

My Dear Brothers and Sisters in Christ,

During April, my son Carlton will be celebrating his birthday. Since Carlton is Downes Syndrome, his party will be the usual cake, ice cream and simple presents. What will we be celebrating?

Life! Carlton's life that has brought us in contact with so many beautiful people doing the Lord's work with the developmentally disabled.

Life! Carlton's life that has lead Carl and me to fight for proper food, health care and schooling for the retarded.

Life! Carlton's life that has caused us to form a parents group which has been so instrumental in making Hilldale a facility worthy of taking care of our children.

Life! Carlton's life that has challenged us to become involved with the dignity of all.

All the ice cream and cake in the world would not be enough to celebrate Carlton!

Yours in Christ
Mimi Smith

What started out as Special Love between Mimi and me has become more special. Carlton, Colleen, Tom and Alicia have made it so. They are the major ingredients of that Special Love. Special Love hasn't stopped growing because the kids have left home. They have taken it with them and passed it along to their children. They show their Special Love to us in other ways now, phone calls, their visits, a success or even a failure. Special Love is grandchildren, Garrett and Justin, Patrick, Max, Thomas, Sadie Ray and Ryan It's a new porch, a greeting card. Sometimes Special Love is just a thought.

I asked Carlton's brother and sisters to help me finish my story by sharing a few of their thoughts about growing up with Carlton. I believe what they have written can best be described as "Special Love."

Colleen:

At a young age my brother Tom and I learned to run interference. We kept Carlton away from a certain corner of the living room where a floor heater lurked behind our nubby green couch. We knew that before pain could slowly crawl up our big brother's spine to alert his brain to hot danger, the smooth metal grate covering that heater might singe waffle prints into the soles of his feet.

Despite his sluggish synapses, Carlton taught me how to be sensitive. By slowly floating his hand just above my skin from wrist to shoulder, he would raise every hair on my arm with some kind of inverse lightning. Reciprocally, whenever my brothers emerged from the barbers' chair, I'd create an electric sensation by skimming my hands over their freshly mown brush cuts.

One of Carlton's most vivid gifts to me was his smile. When my son Max was ten weeks old I took him to visit my big brother. It had probably been years since Carlton had seen, let alone held, a baby. Carlton was sitting cross-legged on his bed. I put Max in his lap and they locked eyes for a tiny eternity that flooded that antiseptic-colored institutional room with quiet awe. Eventually I said, "Carlton, that's my son." My brother looked directly into my eyes and smiled at me with nothing short of brilliance. He was the proudest uncle ever, and I will never forget that radiant smile.

The next time Carlton and Max saw each other Max was seven months old. Carlton rested in his bed, albeit a different one, and I settled Max into his lap again. My characteristically active son lay peacefully alert as he and his uncle dove into each other's eyes to exchange more of the particular awareness that we seem to shed when we acquire language. It sanctified that hospice room.

When Carlton's liver began to fail, my sister Alicia had been the only one home in San Diego. She said that she wanted him moved to hospice, but Carlton's doctor had been utterly baffled as to why. Carlton had tutored my family on the fine points of being human, yet, as we hurtled toward his deathbed, my sister had to defend his humanity to his own physician. She succeeded, and we found him at hospice.

Tom arrived last, and the midnight room was quiet. He entered softly and said, "Carlton, I'm here". Carlton met my brother's gaze with the same serene expression of love that he had shared with my son. My brothers' long visual embrace was punctuated, not by the brush cuts they'd both left behind in childhood, but by Carlton's last act of consciousness – a silent, yet profoundly articulate smile.

Tom:

Growing up with my brother Carlton is what I did. It did not matter to me that he was different than other people, he was my brother and I loved him. Carlton was filled with enthusiasm, love and joy. He silently led people along, teaching them what is *really* important in life. He taught me many important life lessons. Some lessons I may never use again like how to guard your dinner plate by blocking it with your left arm to the point that our evening meal took on the appearance of a chow call at San Quinton. Other lessons I use every day because he taught me tolerance and to accept others for who they are. Like Carlton, I am a teacher and the lessons I learned from my brother of tolerance, acceptance, and joy in life are lessons I pass on to my students. I am able to proclaim these important lessons and it often takes more than one lecture for my students to understand. I am amazed that Carlton was able to silently get the same message across and it only took meeting him one time. I am forever grateful that Carlton was my brother and my teacher.

Alicia:

My brother Carlton was the best secret keeper of all time. You could tell the guy anything and know he would never spill the beans but, there were a few secrets he could not contain. He had pretty much figured out two huge secrets of life and without saying a word he yelled the secrets out loud and clear. First: That people are worth loving despite all their imperfections. People are messed up and everyone you meet is developmentally disabled in one way or another so the best thing to do is just love them. This simple lesson is one that has given me as well as Colleen and Tom the ability to love just about anyone that comes our way. Romantically this can lead to disaster but it sure makes for an interesting array of friends. I can say with 100 percent conviction that this gift of accepting people for who they are and loving them just because has made my life much more exciting than most folks I know.

Second, Carlton greeted life with a huge smile and a sense of humor. Carlton shared the same sense of humor that runs through our family. All of us like a good joke, especially a good practical joke and we do not mind making those we love look foolish. He was funny! When I worked at Hilldale the administration had a rule that if a resident made a mess the staff member that found the mess had to clean it up. Carlton would wander the halls and find me, take my hand and pull me into a room and present me with a mess. A pile of toys, papers scattered, toilets unflushed, food tossed on a wall. As I cleaned up the mess I would grumble and he would sit on the nearest bed crossed legged and clap and make his joyous quacking noise as I firmly told him what I thought. One evening when greeted with an especially messy mess I called him an ass. The night nurse was walking by the door and I was written up for verbal abuse to a resident! This was called a yellow slip. At that point the gloves were off. I would see Carlton coming toward me and would quickly get another staff member to see what he was up to but, one day it finally happened....Carlton was so persistent for my attention I *had* to go with him. He took my hand and led me into a room and he proceeded to run, literally RUN, away quacking. Carlton had stealthily gotten into the linen closet, grab many towels and walked into the nearest bathroom and shoved the towels in the sink and the toilet. He had then flushed and turned on the water and waited until the bathroom, the adjacent bedroom and part of the hall was flooded and then he had searched for and found me! I was greeted with a flood of biblical proportions and I yelled for backup as I started to mop. A few minutes passed and the night nurse (the very same nurse who had written me up for the 'ass' comment) ran into the room, pointed at me and yelled:

"You! Find your brother!"

Room by room we searched. Carlton was missing but echoing through the halls of Hilldale was Carlton's quacking. The quacking seemed to be emanating from the heater vents high up on the walls. Panic set it. He was not in his room. The nurse started to say thing like, "How could he get in the vent?" and "Should we call a heater expert?" By this time the quacking stopped and visions of pulling my brother blackened by soot out of a vent started to fill my head. I entered his friend Lou's room. Lou was sitting in the room in his wheelchair giggling. Under the bed? No. The bathroom? No.

"Quack! Quack! Quack!" It started again and there he was: on top of a clothing locker stark naked with a blow up inner tube (the kind use in a swimming pool for floating) around his waist. The nurse was right behind me. She took my arm and said "Honey, you figure out how to get him down and I will rip up that yellow slip." You can't tell me for a moment Carlton did not know exactly what he was doing!

Carlton's quacking was unique and hilarious, annoying and joyful all at the same time. It was a sound that everyone that knew Carlton came to love. The day my brother died I knew it was a sound I would never hear again. Imagine my utter surprise when my son Tommy began to make the exact same quacking sound at the age of 11! The fact that my son can talk while quacking often makes me happy that Carlton could not form words.

My oldest son Patrick was the only one of my three guys who got to know Carlton. I would take him to visit and he would play with his uncle. Every single time we left he would say the same thing:

"That Uncle Carlton is a CRAZY guy!"

If being crazy means that you are completely yourself and you don't care what other people think. If being crazy means eating as much as you want of whatever you want. If being crazy means you can maintain a sense of humor in the worst of situations. If being crazy means you can give love and be loved in return without saying a word....then we should all be so lucky to be crazy. We should all be so lucky to have a crazy Uncle.

When Carlton ended up in the hospital and I was informed that he was dying I was the only family member in town. My final act of being his sister was to get him into Hospice. I did it by doing what I had seen my parents do for years. I just demanded (with a sweet smile) that he got the care that everyone no matter their mental capacity deserves....and I boldly lied that I had power of attorney and so whatever I said went. I was reminded of the story of the Velveteen Rabbit by Margery Williams that my mother would read to us when we were children. In the story the toy rabbit wants to become real and he seeks wisdom from the toy horse.

"Real isn't how you are made," said the Skin Horse "It is a thing that happens to you. When a child loves you for a long, long time. Not just to play with but REALLY loves you, then you become Real."
"Does it hurt?" asked the Rabbit.
"Sometimes," said the Skin Horse.
"Does it happen all at once, like being wound up," he asked, "or bit by bit?"
'It doesn't happen all at once,' said the Skin Horse. 'You become. It takes a long time. That's why it doesn't happen often to people who break easily, or have sharp edges, or who have to be carefully kept. Generally, by the time you are Real, most of your hair has been loved off, and your eyes drop out and you get loose in the joints and very shabby. But these things don't matter at all, because once you are Real you can't be ugly, except to people who don't understand."
— Margery Williams, *The Velveteen Rabbit*

My brother Carlton was born broken. The opposite of the Rabbit, he was born Real and he made all those that loved him Real. By the end of his story Carlton was bald, and missing teeth, his skin was different shades of white and olive due to Alopecia. He had no eyebrows or eyelashes and he was beautiful because I understood him. Doctors would come into the room and back up shocked, and stunned into stammering but

I helped them understand my brother. I would smile and introduce them to Carlton and say "I know he doesn't look like much but he has changed more hearts and minds then most people you will ever meet." By the end of our interaction they were willing to move mountains of red-tape to get Carlton what he deserved, and they did. From the doctor that smiled at me and winked as he stated, "Power of Attorney huh?" to the Hospice nurse who upon the suggestion of Colleen and I brought every single desert Hospice had into Carlton's room because 'If this is the last thing he eats it really should be dessert' (it was indeed the last thing he ate). Hearts and minds were changed up until the very end. Carlton died with my mom in a room at the beautiful Hospice building high on a hill in San Diego. As he slipped away the song "Celebration" came on the radio. Up until his very last breath Carlton got what we all want: a caring family, good friends, lots of our favorite food, contentment, inner peace love and a song of celebration when it is all over. Without spending a cent, without a car or a house or fancy clothes without any material possessions it was his and he got it *all* without saying a single word.

Made in the USA
San Bernardino, CA
02 December 2014